Side by Side

21 Duets for the Beginning Pianist

By Ted Cooper and Amy Glennon

Dedicated to our parents:
Betty and Glen Cooper
Sylvia and Glenn Glennon

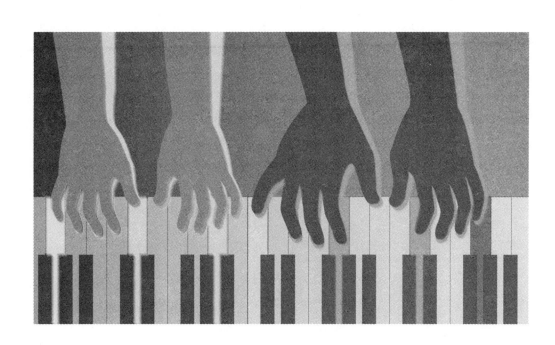

© 1994 Summy-Birchard Music
division of Summy-Birchard Inc.
All Rights Reserved   Printed in U.S.A.

Summy-Birchard Inc., exclusively distributed by
Warner Bros. Publications
15800 N.W. 48th Avenue, Miami, FL 33014

Any duplication, adaptation or arrangement of the compositions
contained in this collection requires the written consent of the Publisher.
No part of this book may be photocopied or reproduced in any way without permission.
Unauthorized uses are an infringement of the U.S. Copyright Act and are punishable by law.

Preface

There is nothing more exciting than a young child fully expressing a musical idea. This collection provides a variety of musical experiences that encourage expressive playing from the beginning. *Side by Side* is designed to coordinate with *Time to Begin*, the first book of the *Music Tree* series, but can be used with any interval-based reading method. The music in this volume uses three basic reading styles:

Off-Staff Notation (pages 4–9)	The student's position is found from a key-board legend.
Partial-Staff Notation (pages 10–18)	The first note is named and then the student reads by interval.
Grand Staff (pages 19–24)	The student finds the position by reading landmarks Middle C, Treble G, and Bass F.

All the pieces in off-staff and partial-staff notation can be played as solos beginning in any octave. When played with the accompaniment, the correct starting position is shown with the teacher's part.

We express our deep appreciation to Frances Clark and Louise Goss, who have shaped our lives both in and out of the studio and whose tireless search for excellence continues to be an inspiration.

We also offer our sincere thanks to our students and colleagues at the New School for Music Study (Princeton, NJ) and Mount Holyoke College (South Hadley, MA) for their support and encouragement in the development of this project. We are especially grateful to Michelle Aalders, Marcy Castro, Noriko Schneiderman, and Allan Watt for their valuable input.

—Ted Cooper and Amy Glennon

Contents

Jumbo

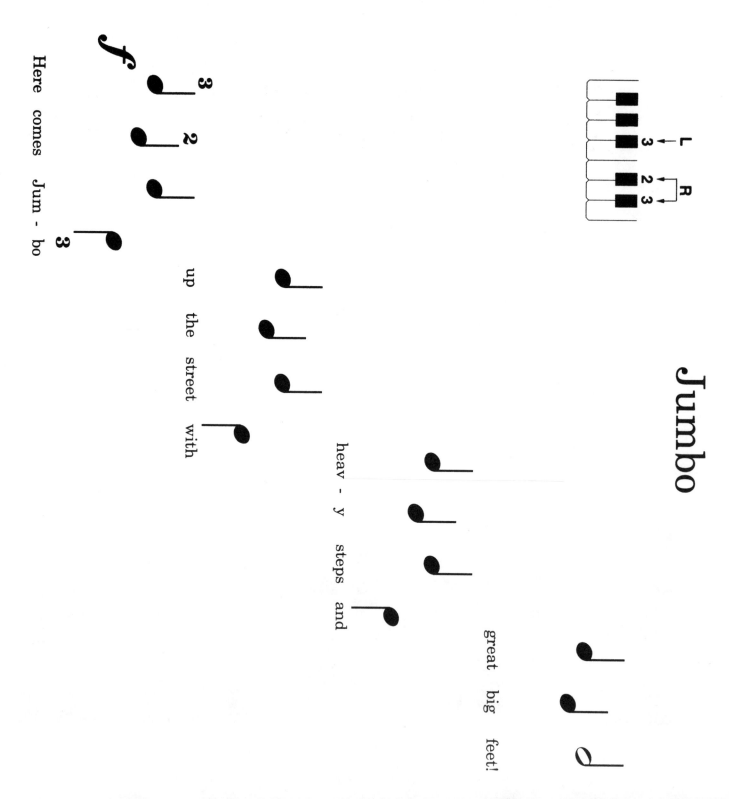

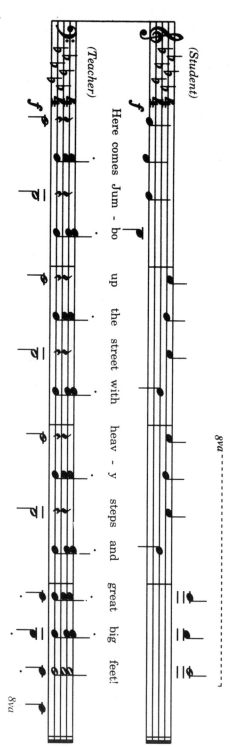

(Student)

(Teacher)

Here comes Jum - bo up the street with heav - y steps and great big feet!

Here comes Jum - bo up the street with heav - y steps and great big feet!

Echo

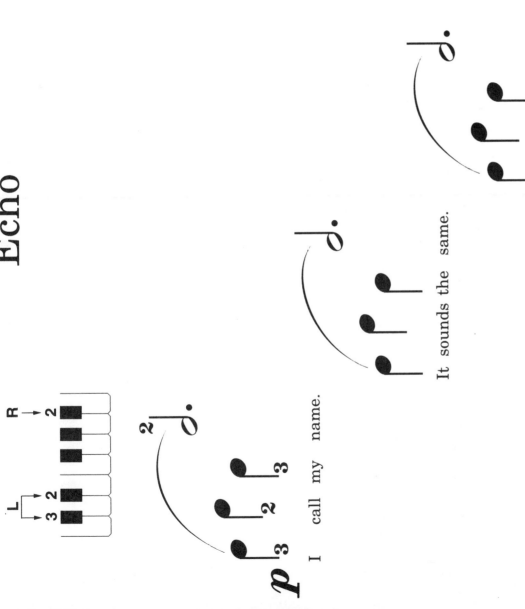

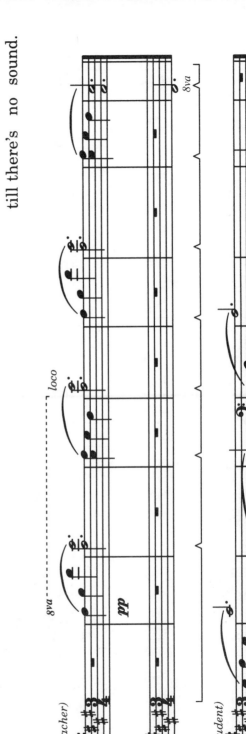

Hide and Seek

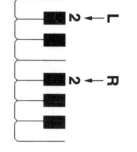

Hide and go seek! Count- ing to ten.

Hide and go seek!

No - one can peek! Hi - ding a - gain!

No - one can peek!

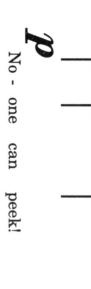

(Student)

Hide and go seek! No-one can peek! Count-ing to ten. Hi - ding a - gain!

(Teacher)

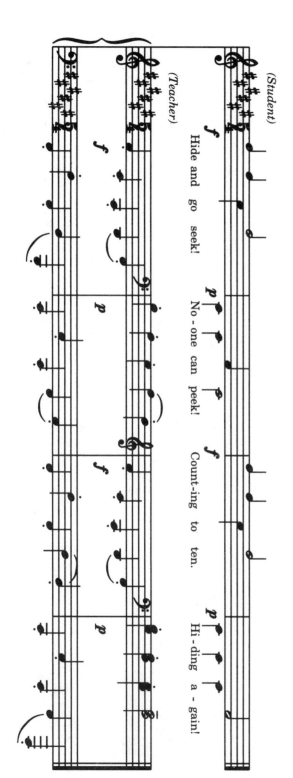

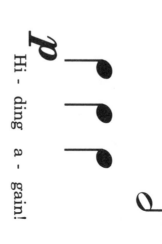

Tag

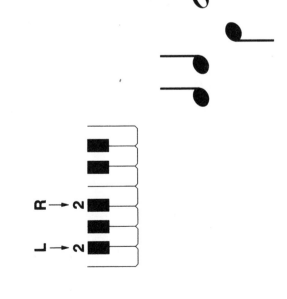

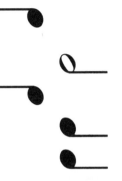

Play- ing tag, she's "it,"

Bet- ter not stay!

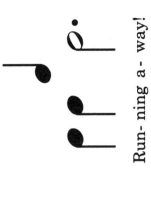

Play- ing tag, he's "it,"

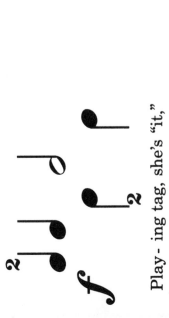

Run- ning a - way!

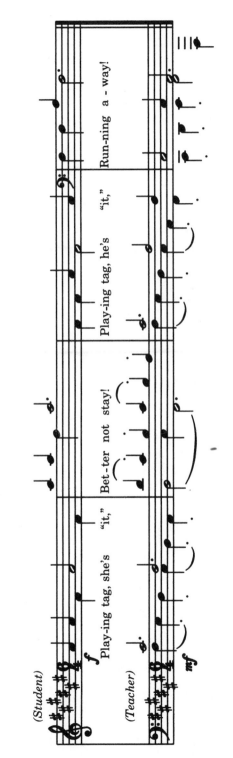

The Juggler

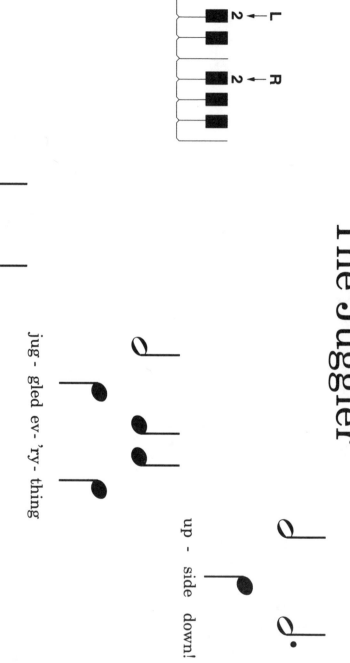
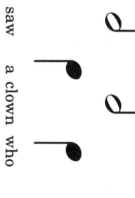

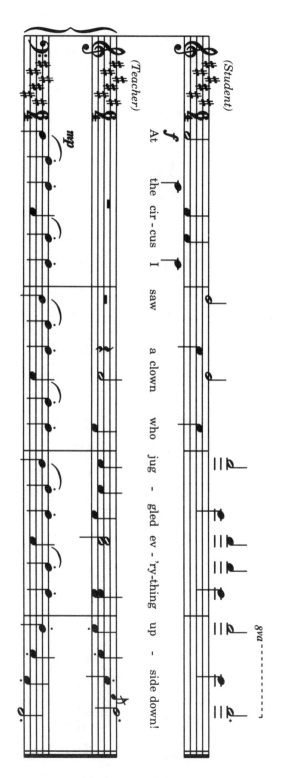

At the cir-cus I saw a clown who jug-gled ev-'ry-thing up - side down!

(Student)

(Teacher)

At the cir-cus I saw a clown who jug - gled ev - 'ry-thing up - side down!

Autumn Leaves

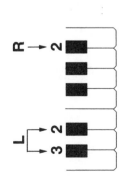

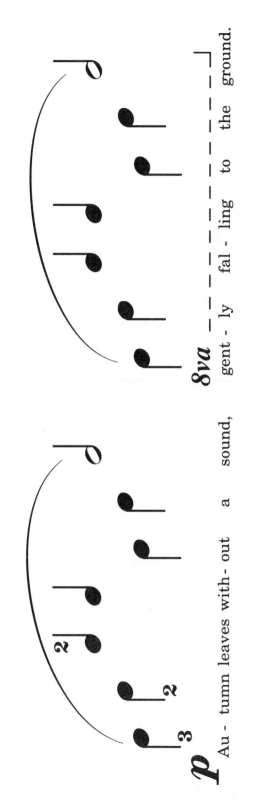

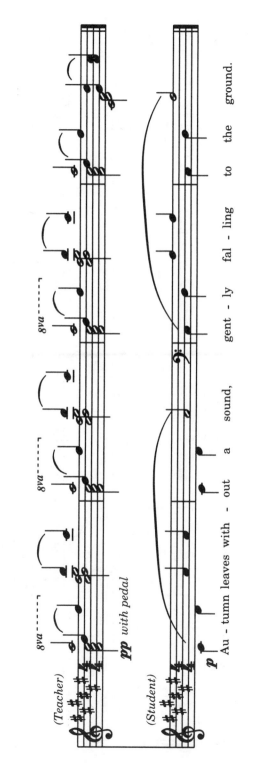

Rocking Chair

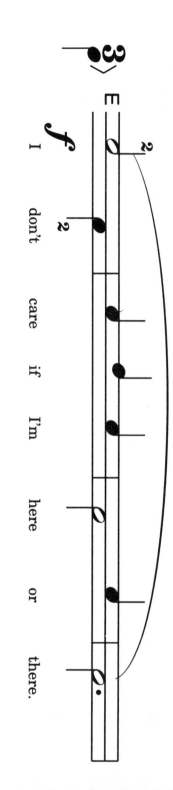

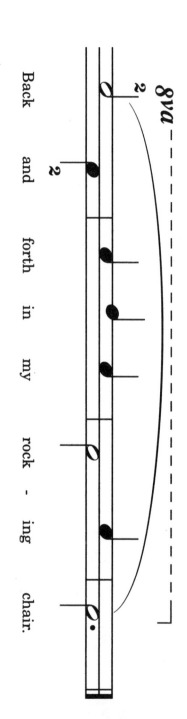

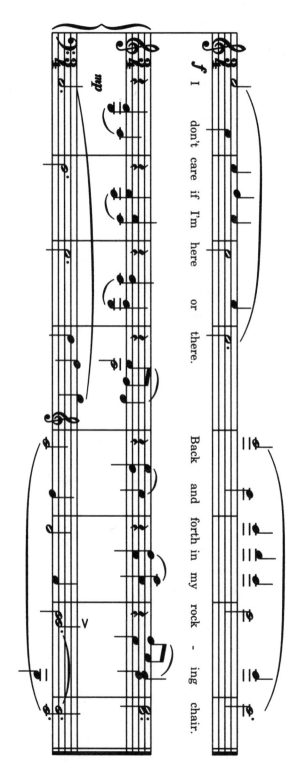

10

I Like Jazz

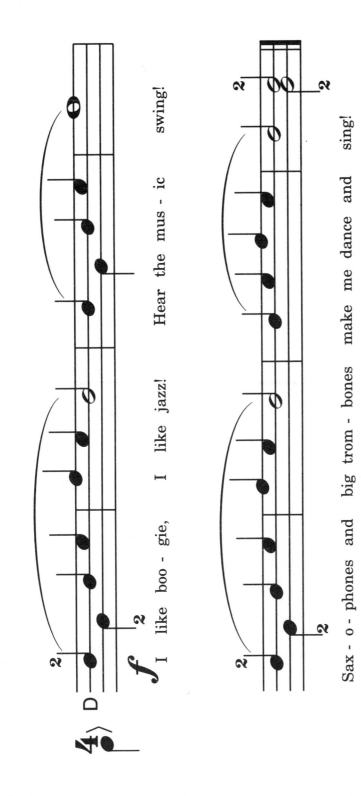

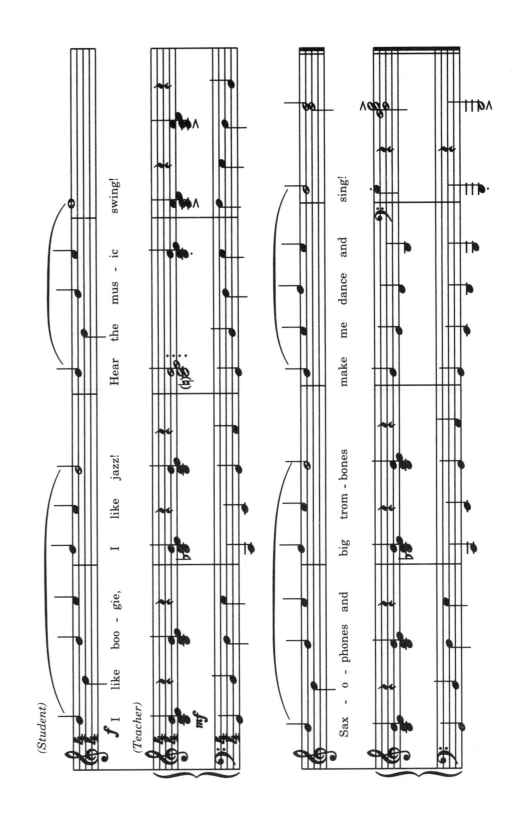

Lullaby

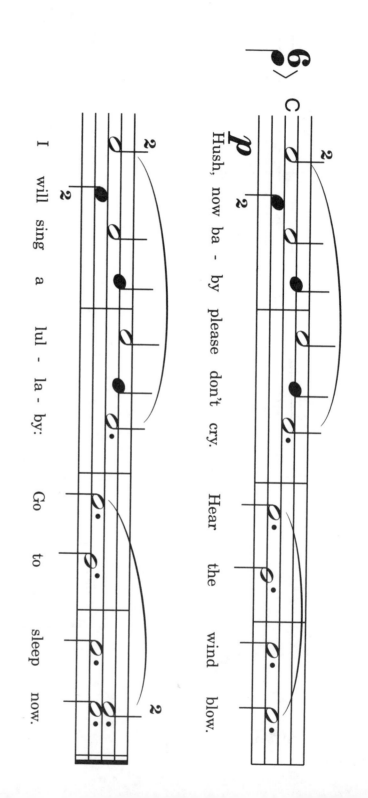

New Friend

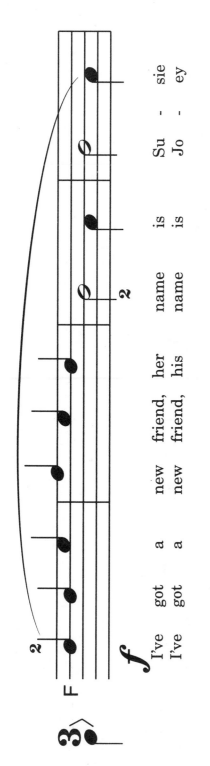

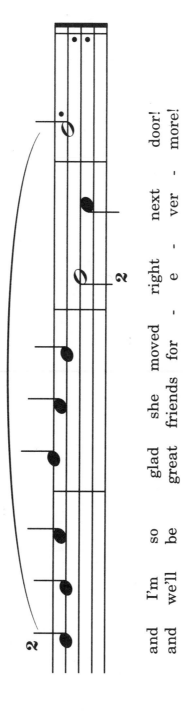

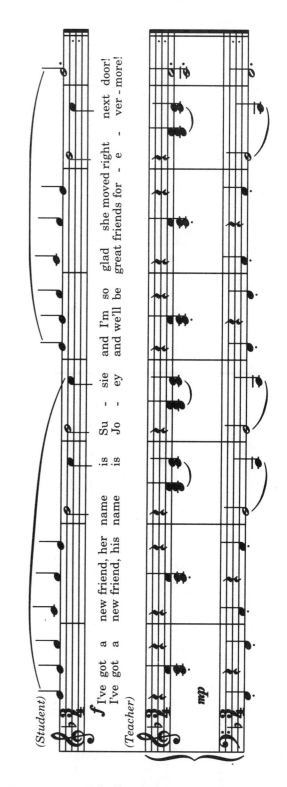

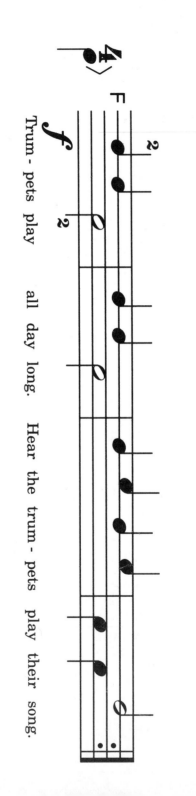

Trumpets

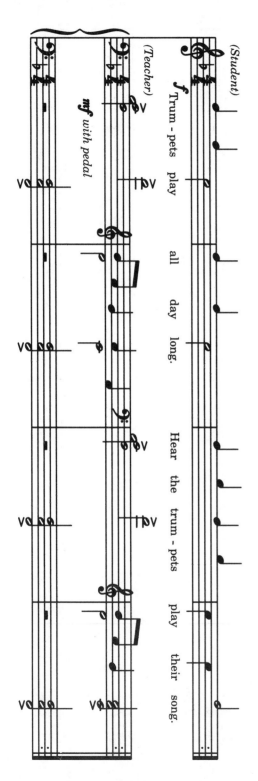

Looking Up

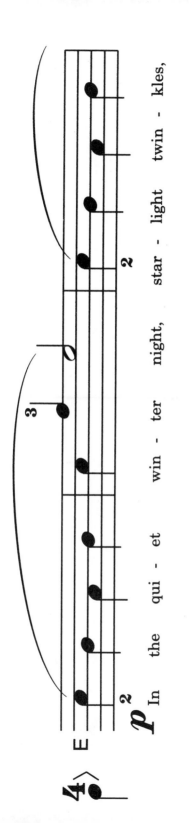
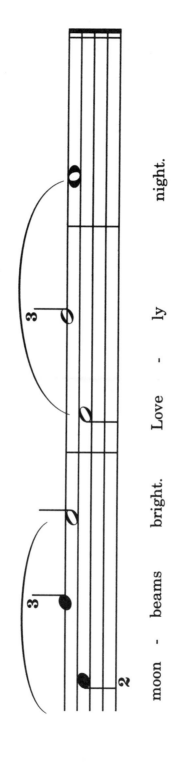
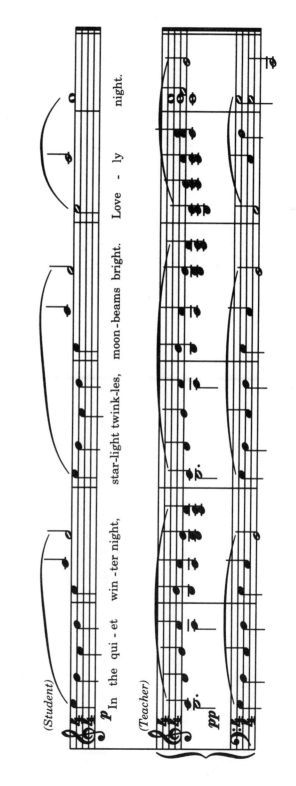

Drum and Flute

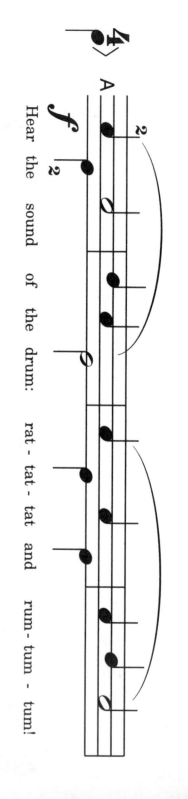

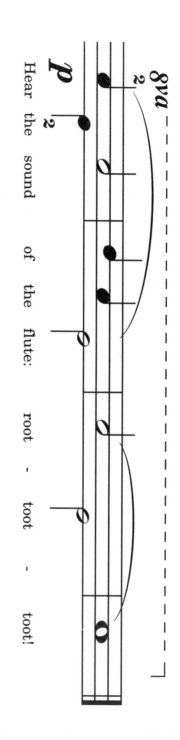

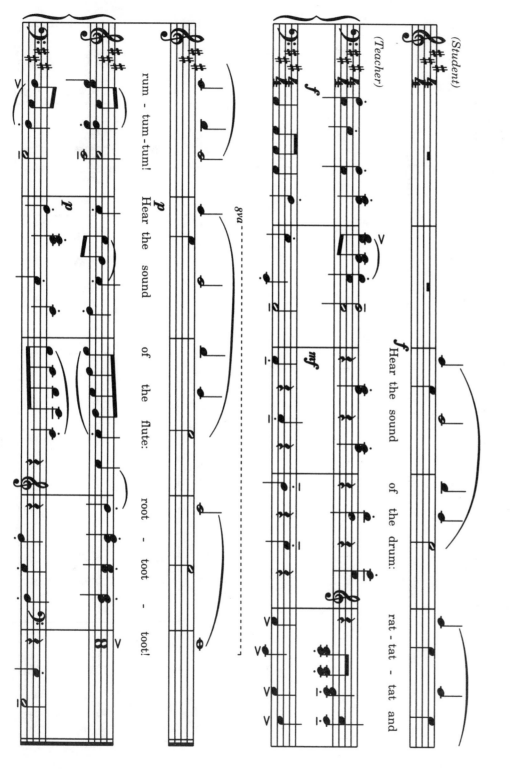

Mermaid

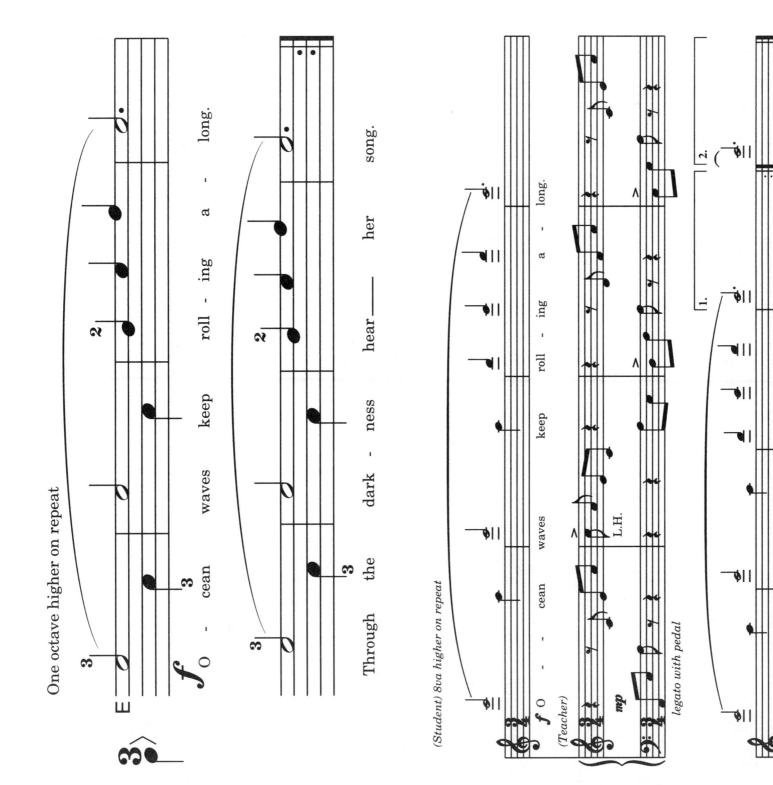

Shoe Trouble

3

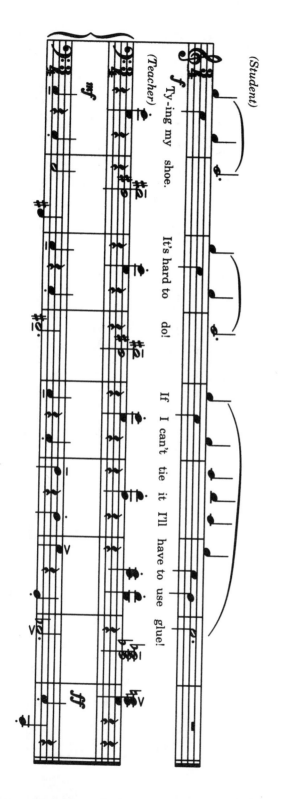

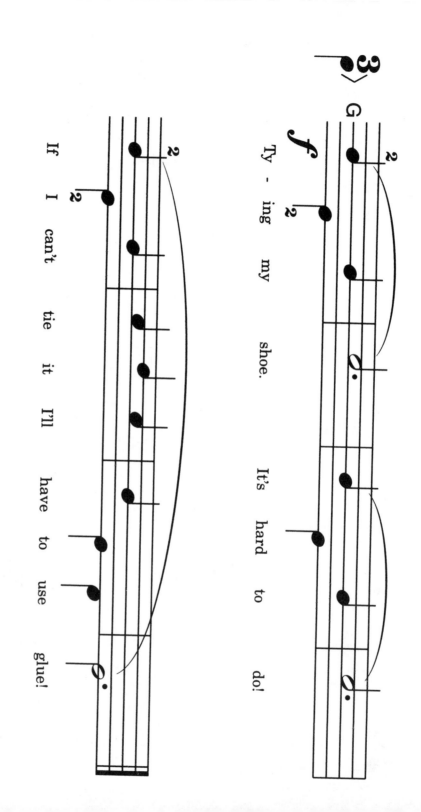

Dark Hallway

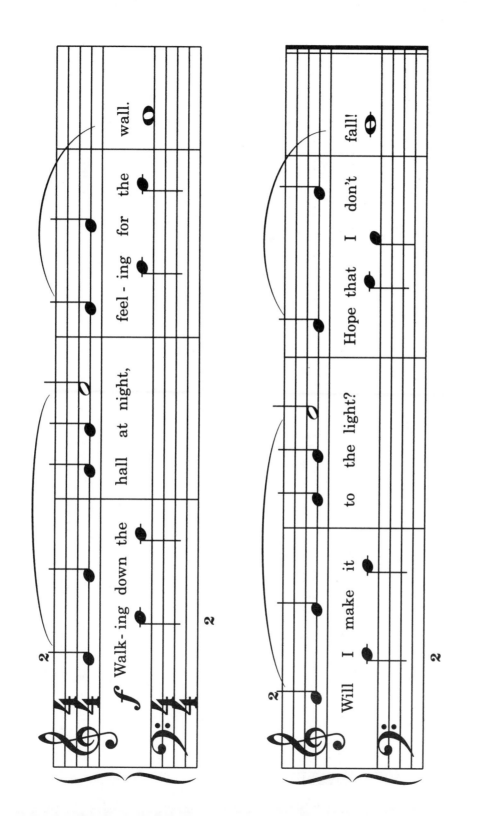

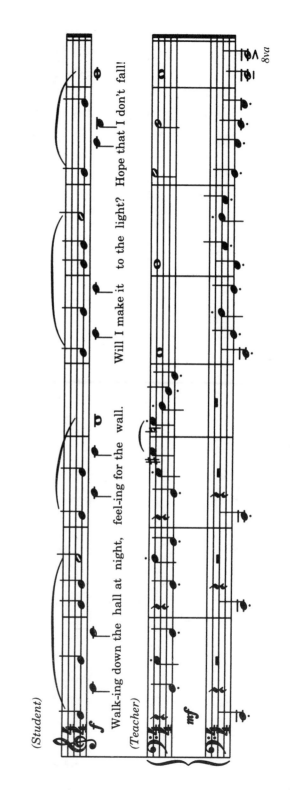

Mountains

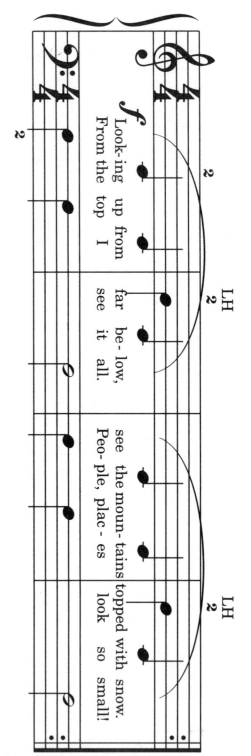

f Look-ing up from far be-low,
From the top I see it all.

see the moun-tains topped with snow.
Peo-ple, plac - es look so small!

LH 2

From the top I see it all.
Look-ing up from far be-low,

Peo-ple, plac - es look so small!
see the moun-tains topped with snow.

LH 2

(Teacher) Both hands one octave higher throughout.

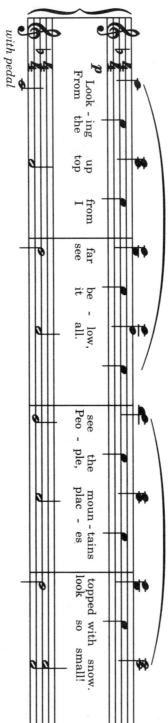

with pedal

p Look-ing up from I see it be-low,
From the top it all.

see the moun-tains topped with snow.
Peo-ple, plac - es look so small!

Tuning Up

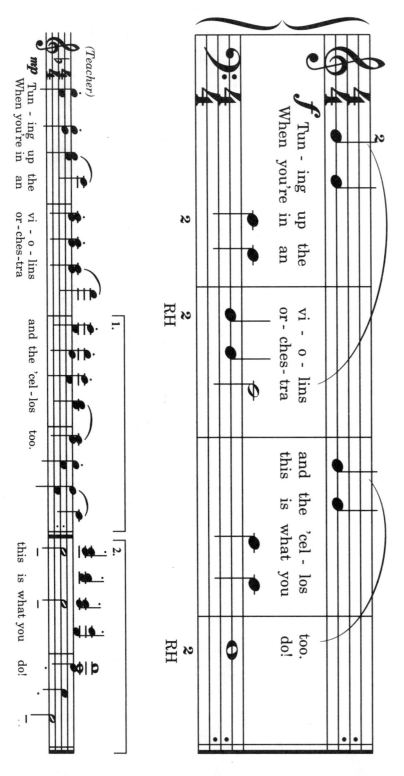

f Tun - ing up the vi - o - lins and the 'cel - los too.
When you're in an or - ches - tra this is what you do!

RH 2

RH 2

(Teacher)

mp Tun - ing up the vi - o - lins and the 'cel - los too.
When you're in an or - ches - tra this is what you do!

1.

2.

this is what you do!

Row, Row, Row Your Boat

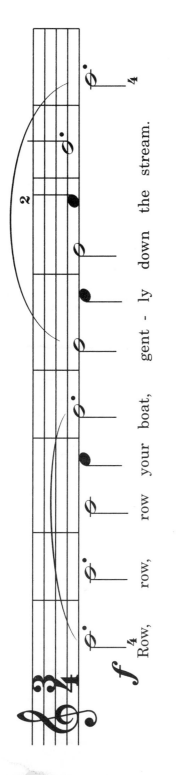
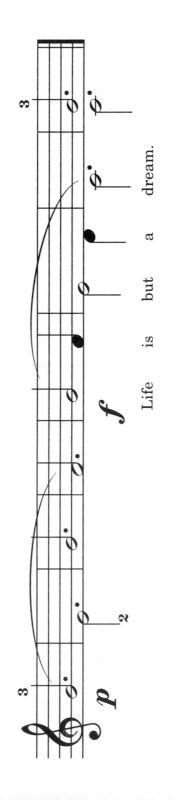
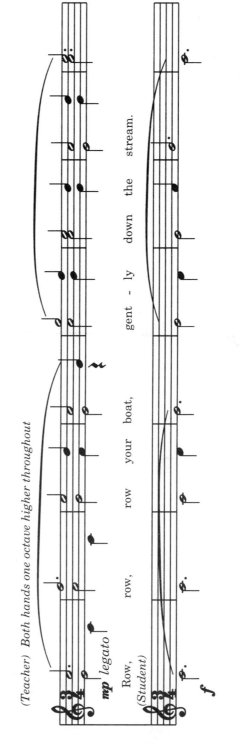
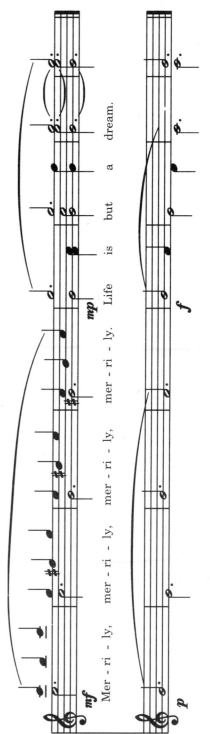

This Old Man

(Teacher)

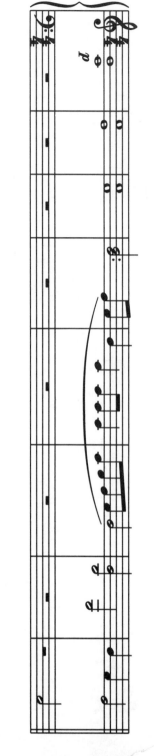

Var. 1

Var. 2

Var. 3

Var. 4

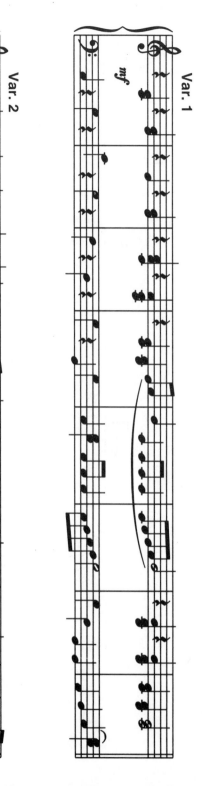

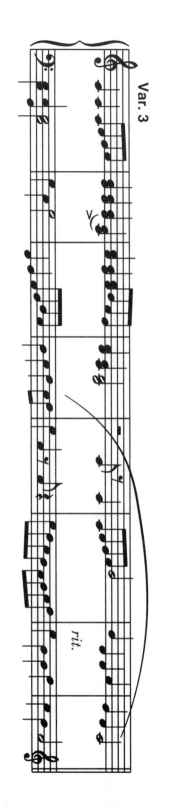

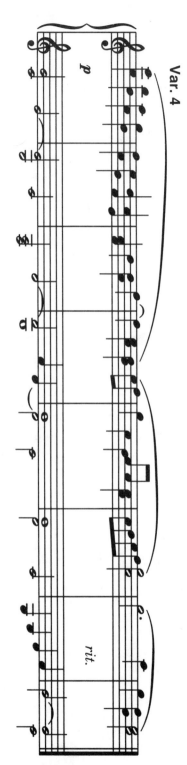

This Old Man

(Student)

One octave higher with duet; last verse, 2 octaves higher.

This old man, he played one, He played knick - knack on my thumb.

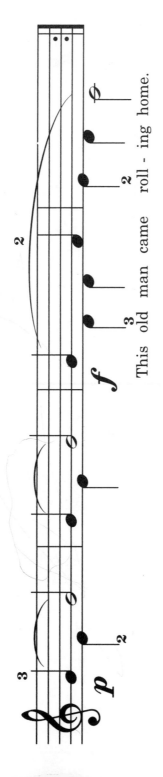

This old man came roll - ing home.

This old man, he played one,
He played knick-knack on my thumb.
With a knick-knack paddy whack, give the dog a bone,
This old man came rolling home.

This old man, he played two,
He played knick-knack on my shoe…

This old man, he played three,
He played knick knack on my knee…

This old man, he played four,
He played knick-knack on my door…

This old man, he played five,
He played knick-knack on my hive…

This old man, he played six,
He played knick-knack with some sticks…

This old man, he played seven,
He played knick-knack up in heaven…

This old man, he played eight,
He played knick-knack on my pate…

This old man, he played nine,
He played knick-knack on my spine…

This old man, he played ten,
He played knick-knack once again.
With a knick-knack paddy whack, give the dog a bone,
This old man came rolling home.

Twinkle, Twinkle Little Star

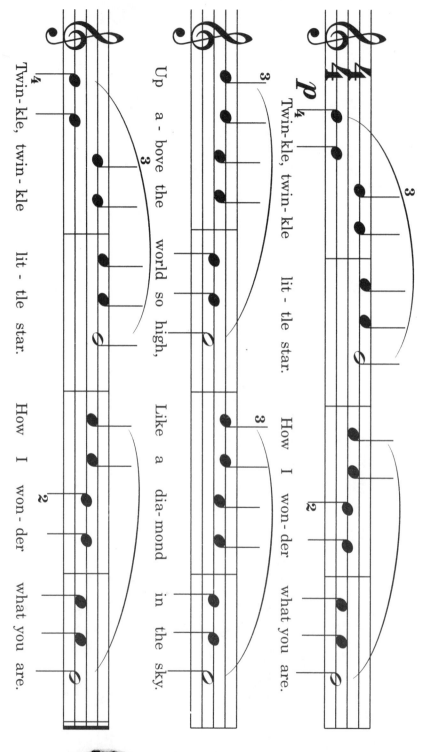

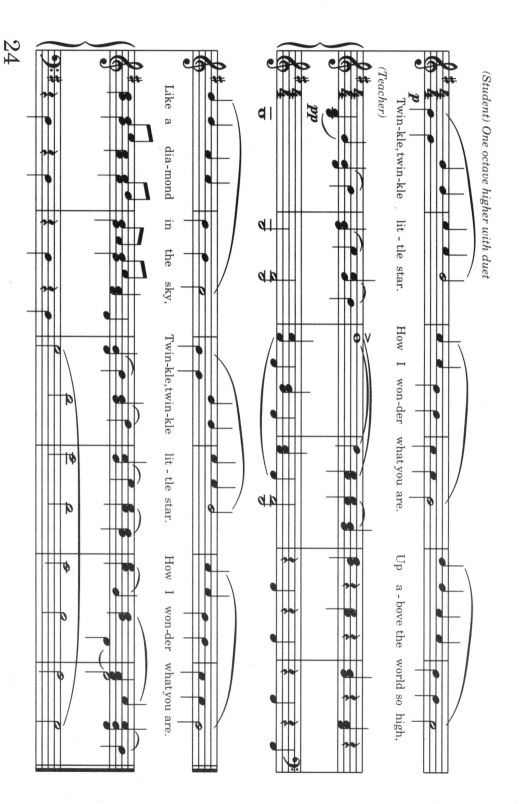

How to Draw

Birds

In Simple Steps

First published in Great Britain 2008

Search Press Limited
Wellwood, North Farm Road,
Tunbridge Wells, Kent TN2 3DR

Reprinted 2009, 2010

Text copyright © Polly Pinder, 2008

Design and illustrations copyright © Search Press Ltd. 2008

All rights reserved. No part of this book, text, photographs or illustrations may be reproduced or transmitted in any form or by any means by print, photoprint, microfilm, microfiche, photocopier, internet or in any way known or as yet unknown, or stored in a retrieval system, without written permission obtained beforehand from Search Press.

ISBN: 978-1-84448-354-9

Readers are permitted to reproduce any of the drawings or paintings in this book for their personal use, or for the purposes of selling for charity, free of charge and without the prior permission of the Publishers. Any use of the drawings or paintings for commercial purposes is not permitted without the prior permission of the Publishers.

Printed in Malaysia

Dedication

*To my dear friend Louise
and her cheeky parrot Rocky*

Illustrations

How to Draw
Birds
In Simple Steps
Polly Pinder

Search Press

Introduction

Birds are an intrinsic part of the natural world. Their habits are fascinating to observe, their calling songs range from exquisite to strangely endearing and the colour of their beautiful, diverse plumage is one of the wonders of the world.

In the following pages I show how to draw a variety of birds using a method in which simple shapes evolve, stage by stage, into the unmistakable form of specific birds. One of the advantages of drawing this way is that the angle of the bird's head and body is captured immediately during the first step, because you start off with basic, simple shapes rather than the complex image of the whole bird.

Each drawing has five stages and two colours are used to make sequences easier to follow. In the first stage I use brown to show the basic geometric shapes of the head, body and tail. In the second stage these simple shapes become turquoise and brown is used to show the new details. In the third stage the previous drawing changes to turquoise and brown is used again for the new details. In the fourth stage more new brown details are added, together with shading which helps to develop the three-dimensional aspect of the bird. The fifth stage is drawn using a graphite pencil and a final image shows the bird painted in its natural colours.

When you are following the stages use an HB, B or a 2B pencil. Draw lightly so that any initial, unwanted lines can be erased easily. Your final work can be a detailed pencil drawing, as shown, or the pencil lines can be drawn over using a technical pen, a ballpoint pen or a felt-tipped pen. Gently erase the original pencil lines at this point.

Once you feel more confident about your drawing, you may want to introduce colour. I have used watercolour, but pencil crayons, felt-tipped pens or pastels also create good effects.

I hope you will draw all the birds here and then go on to do more, perhaps from your own photographs. Using tracing paper to transfer details, lines and shapes to your drawing will make the process a little easier. Once you become familiar with the general anatomy of these beautiful birds, you will soon develop your own style of drawing.

Happy drawing!

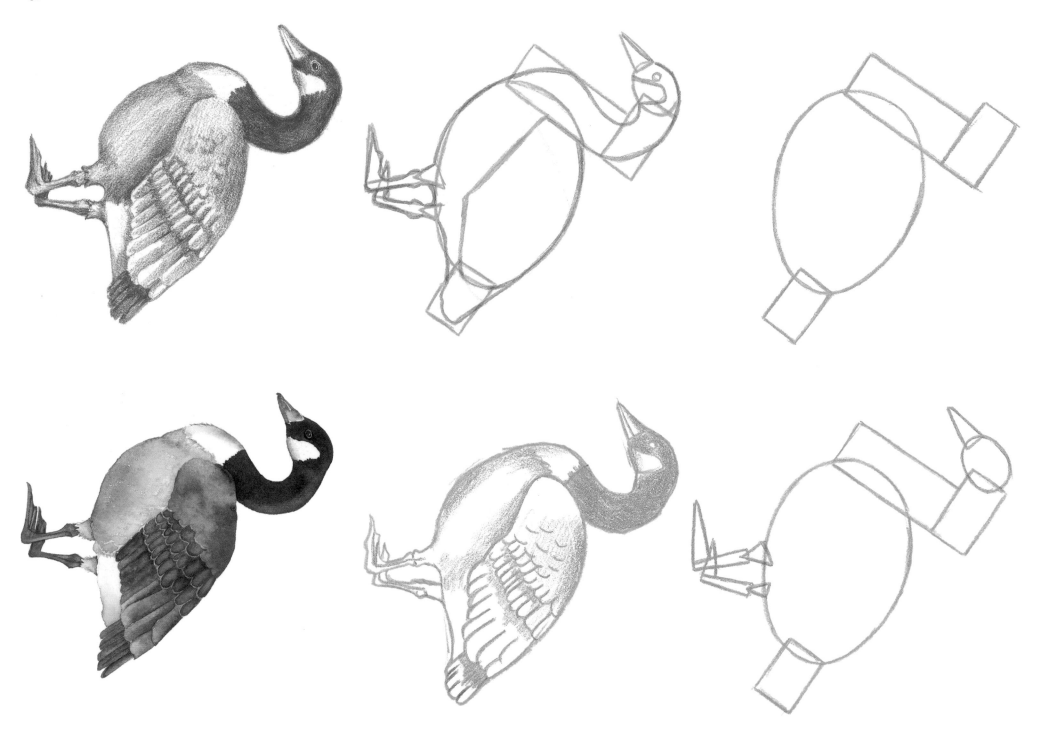

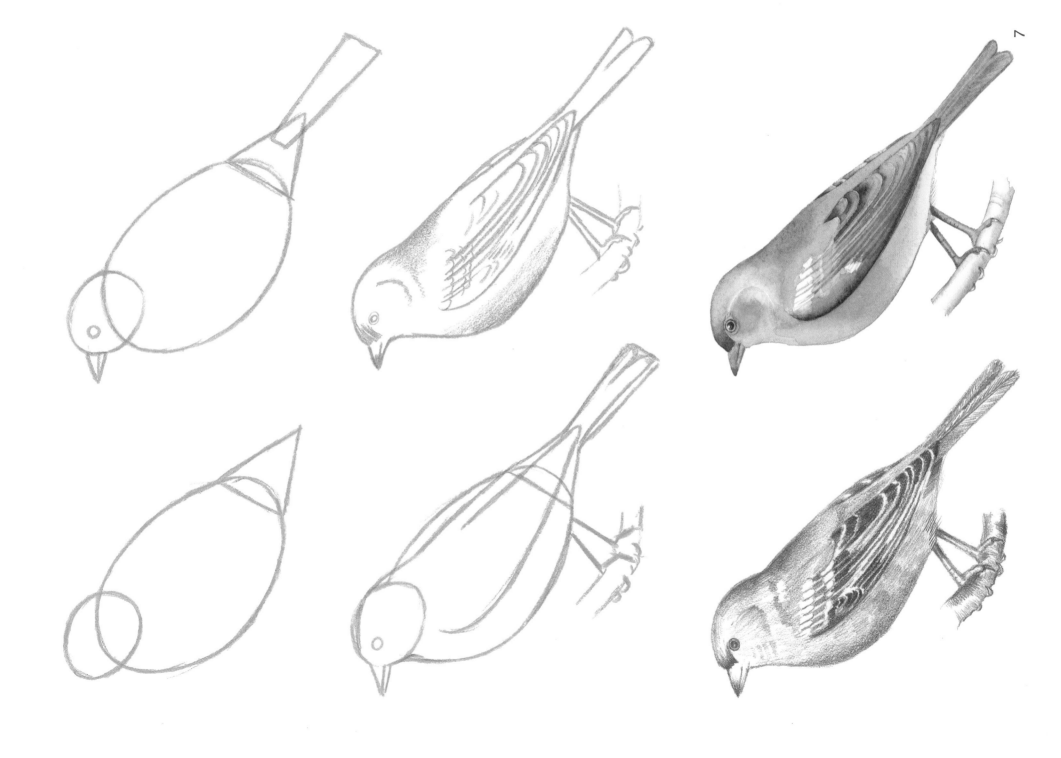

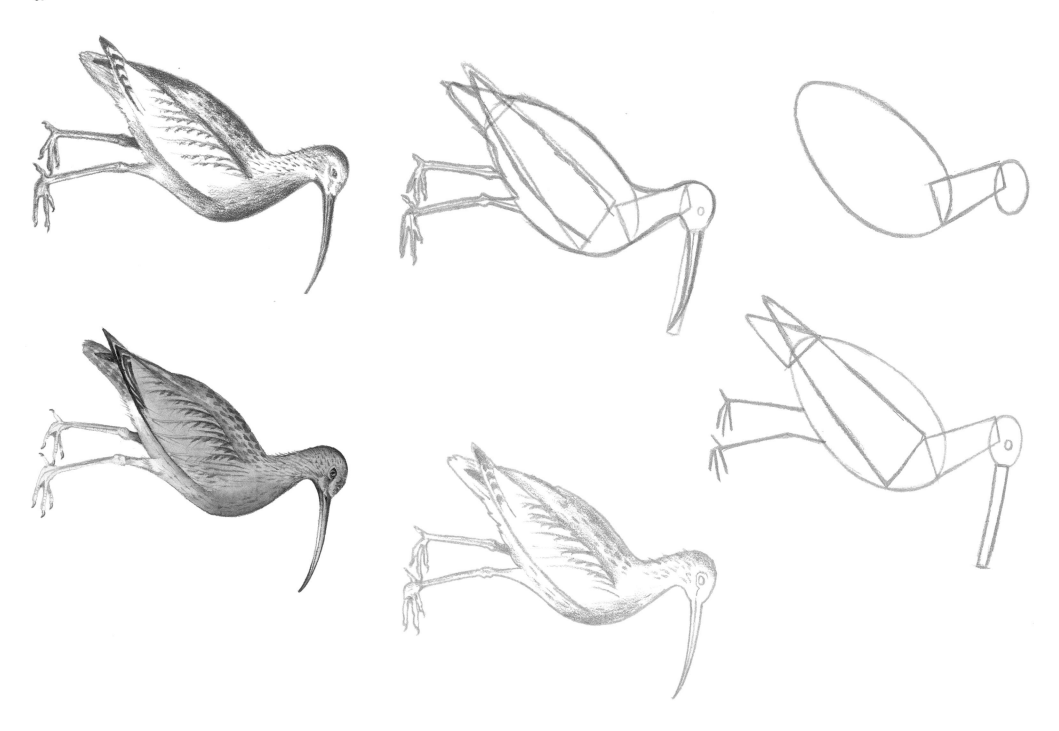

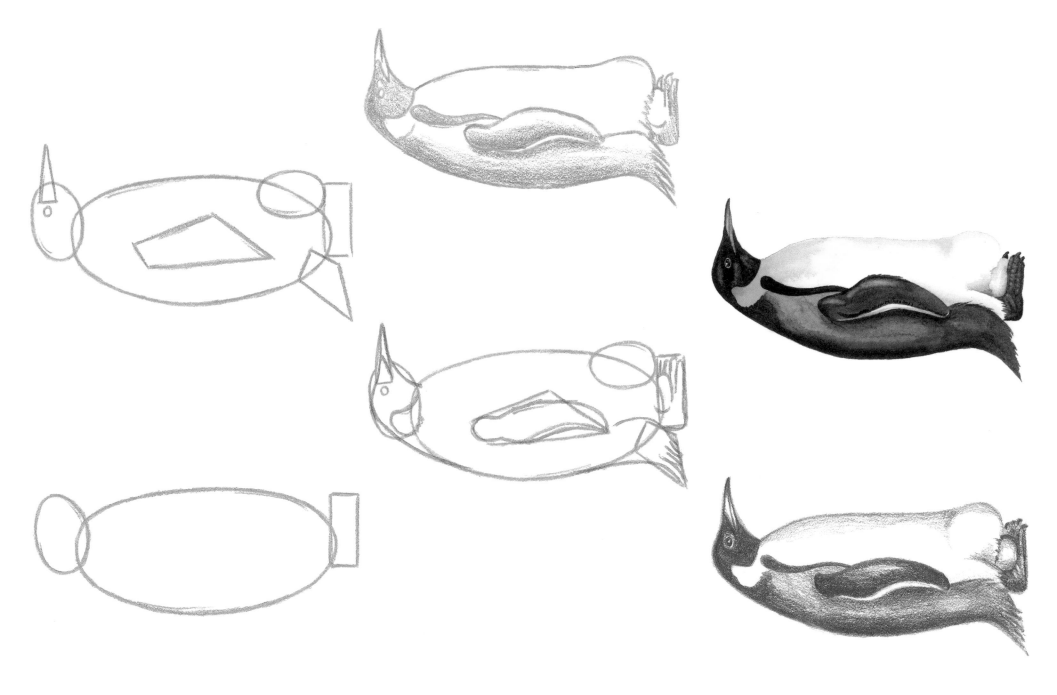

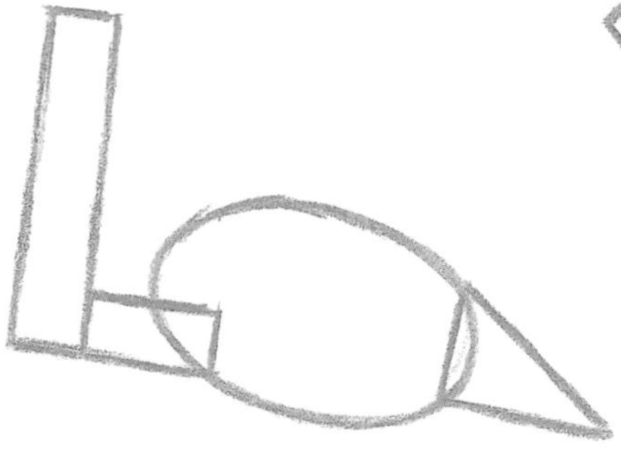

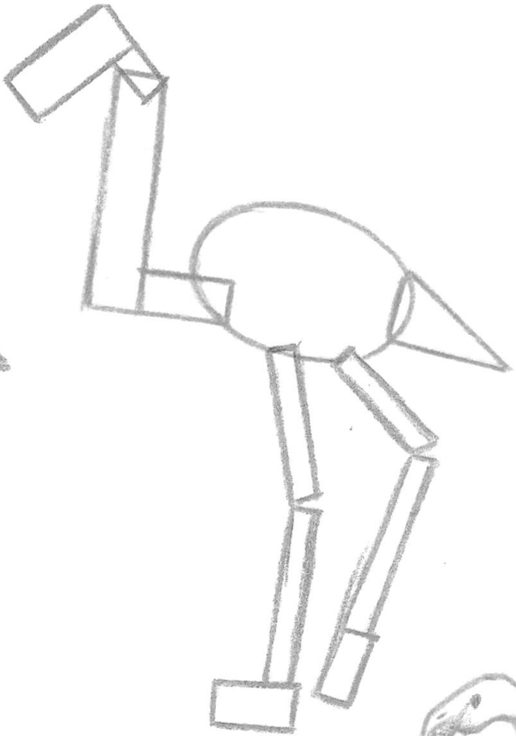

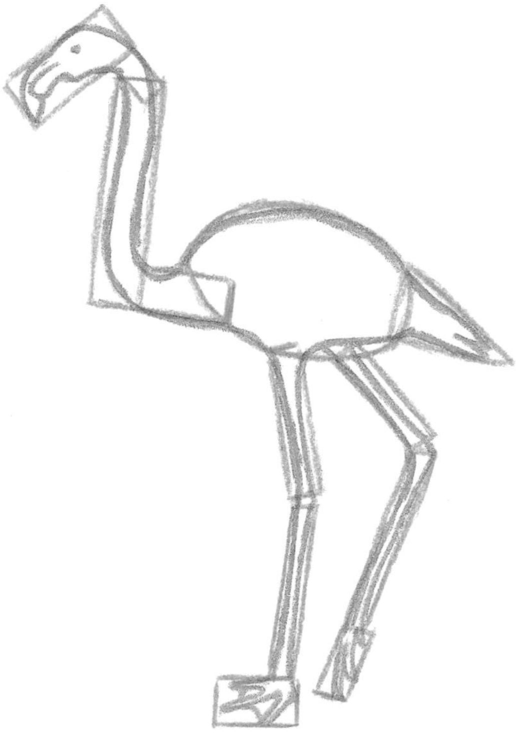

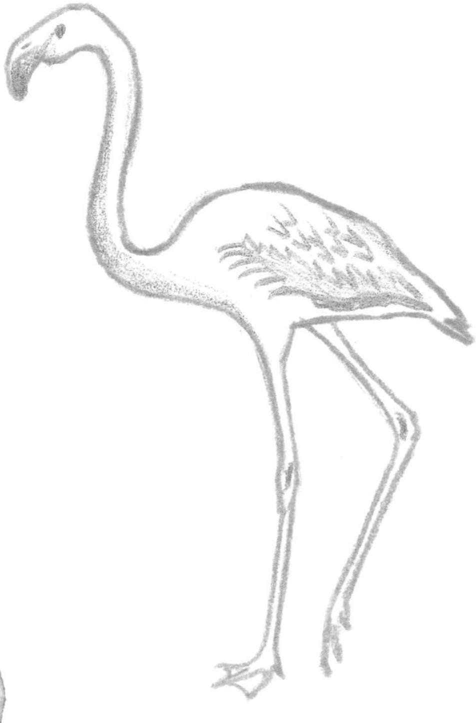

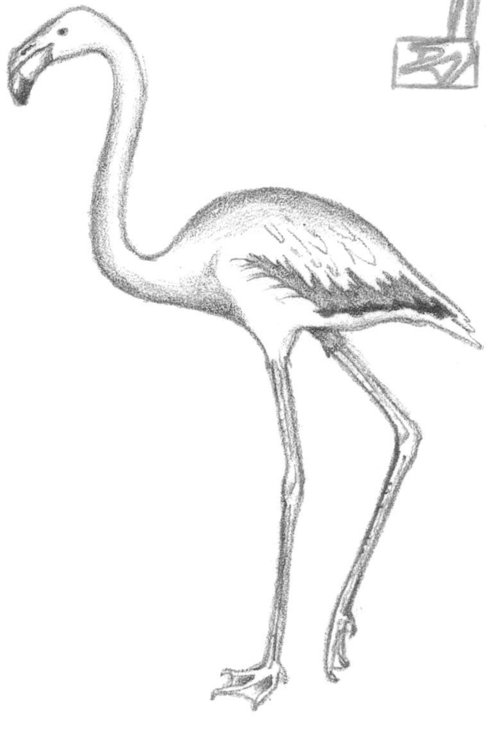

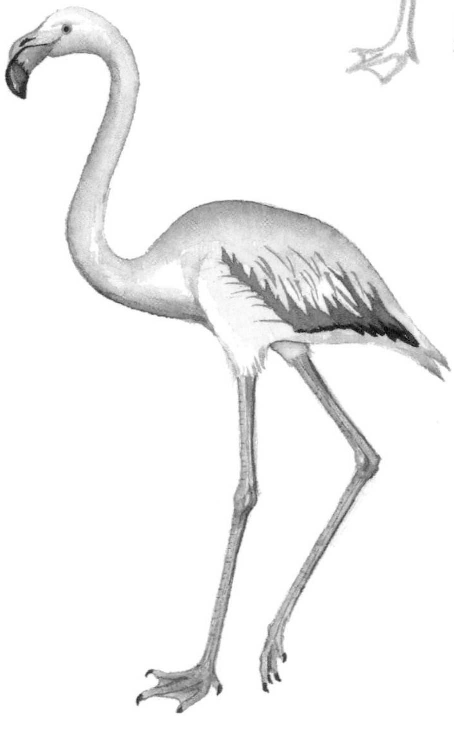

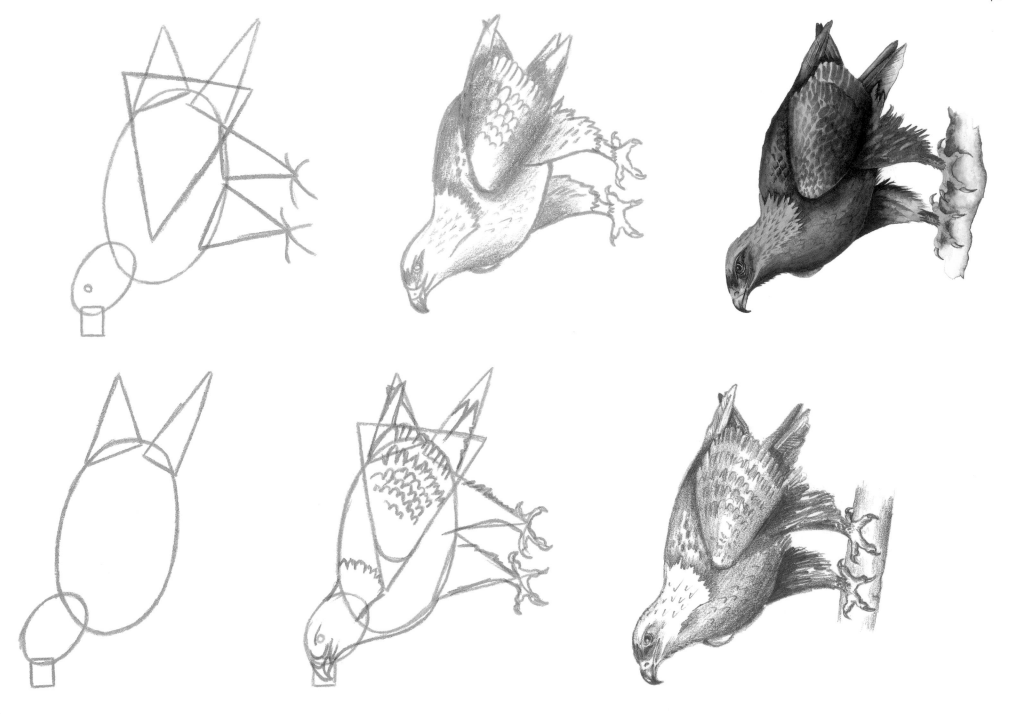

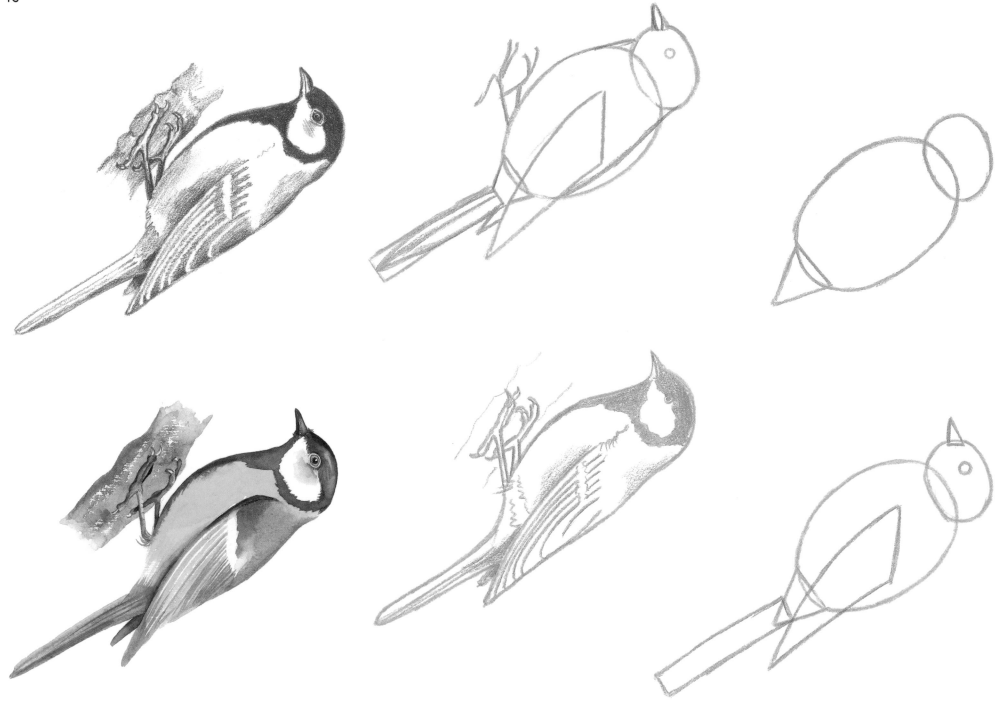

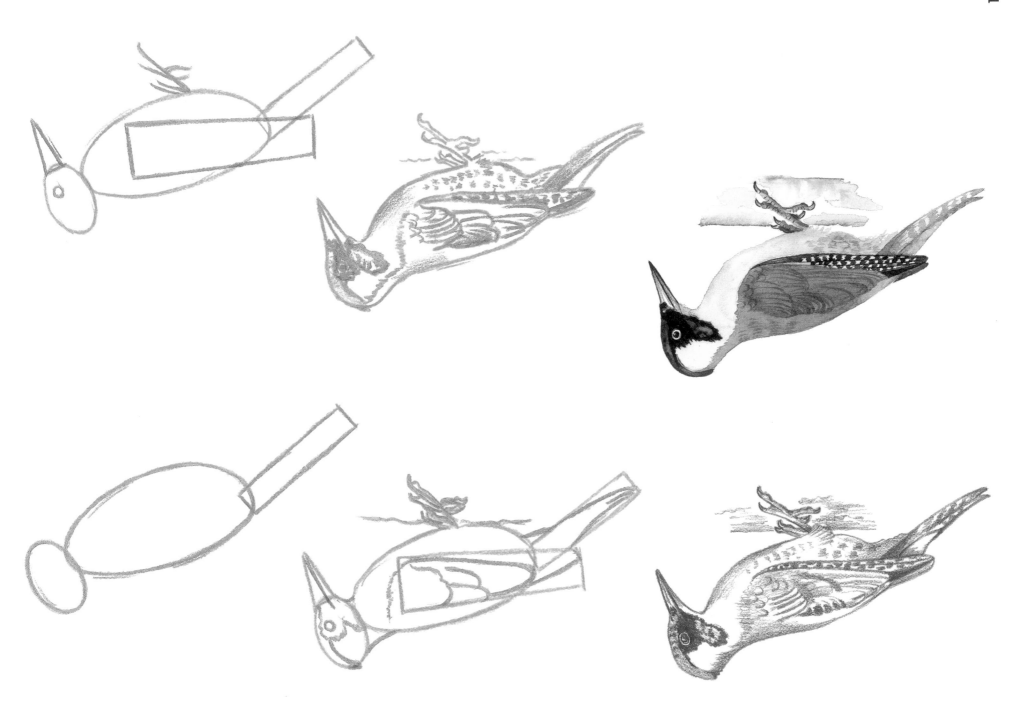

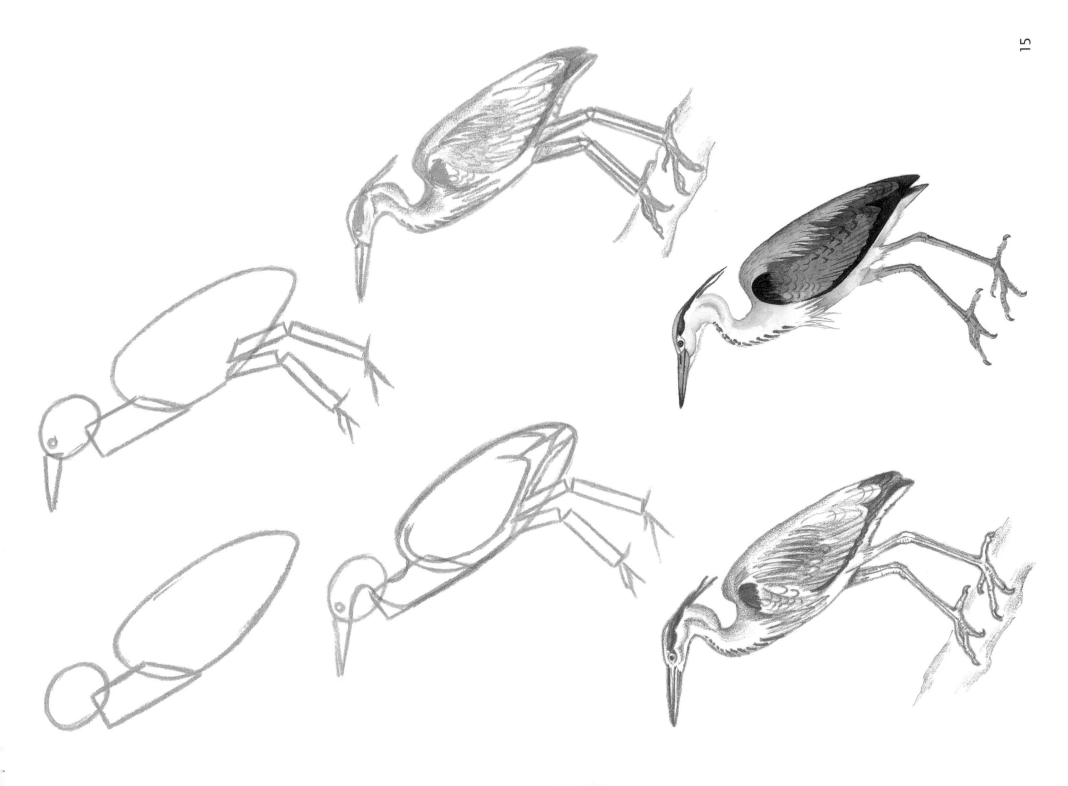

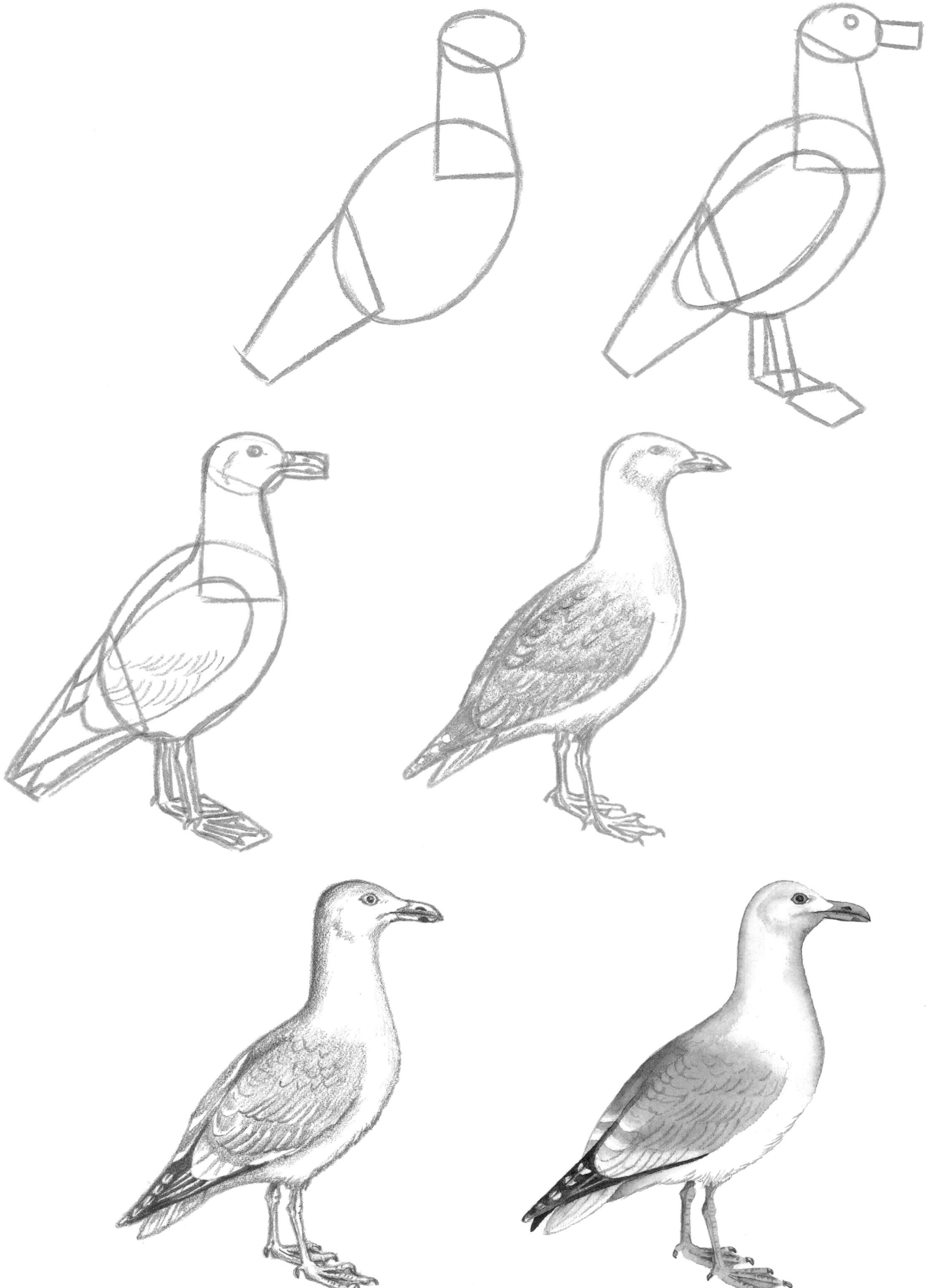

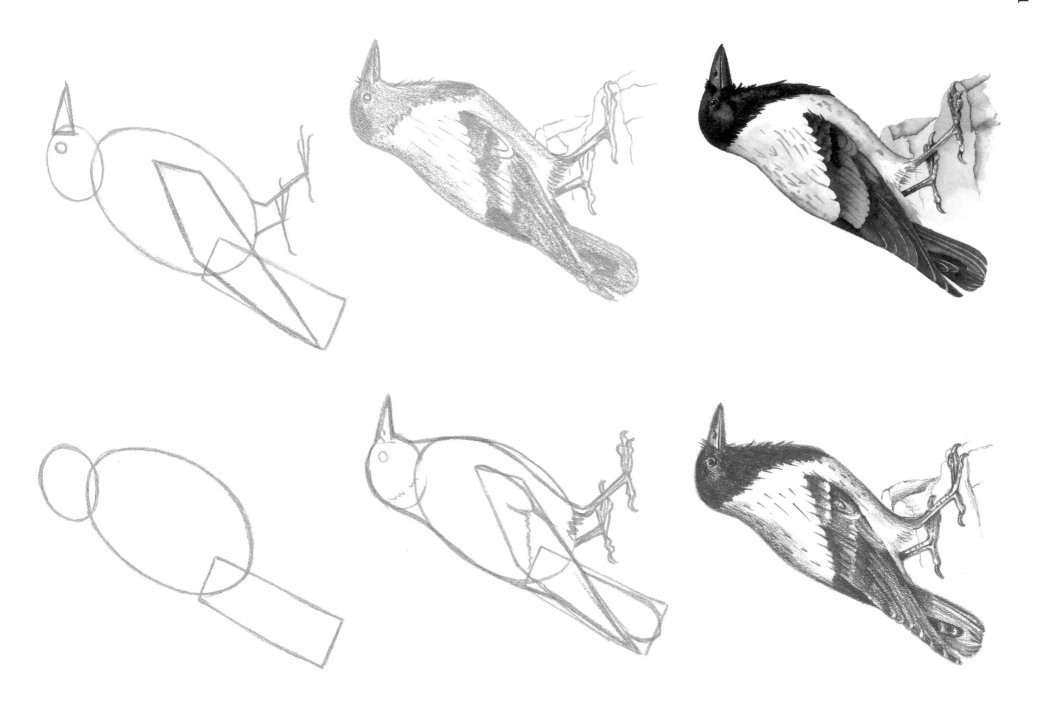

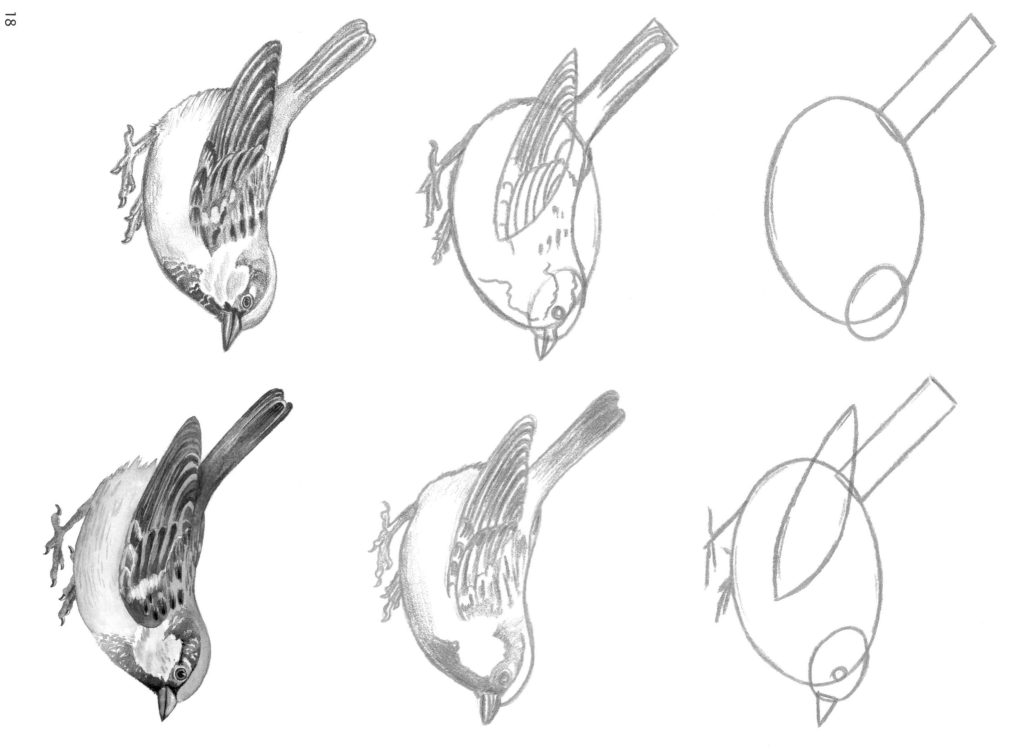

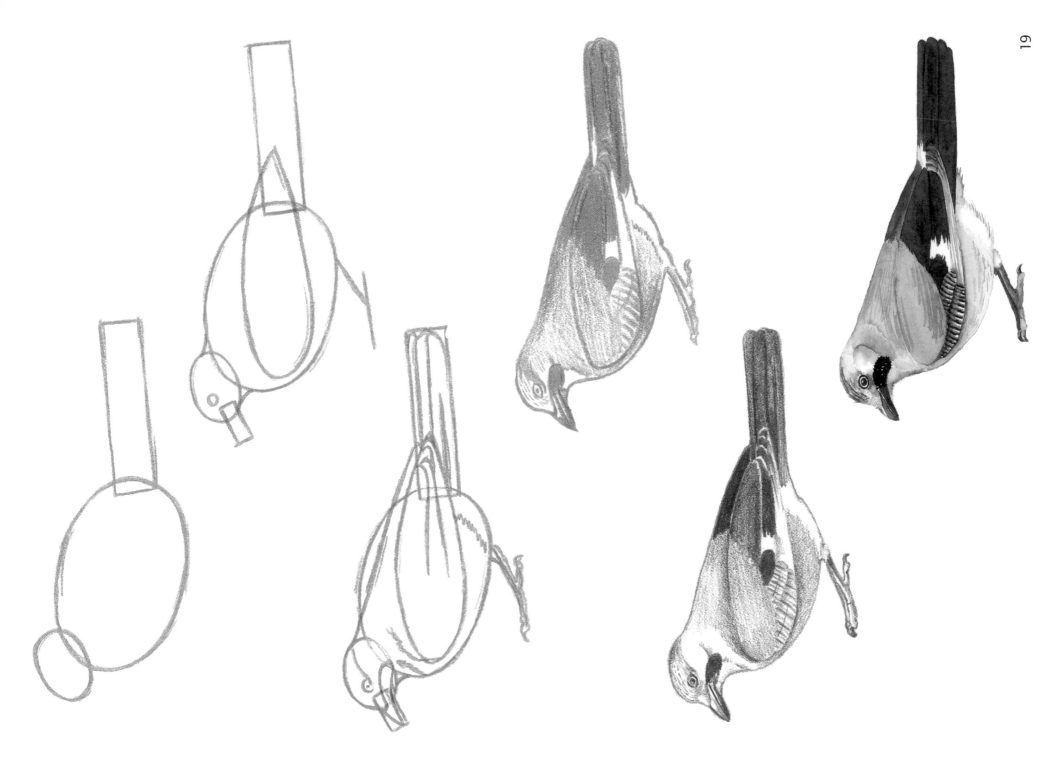

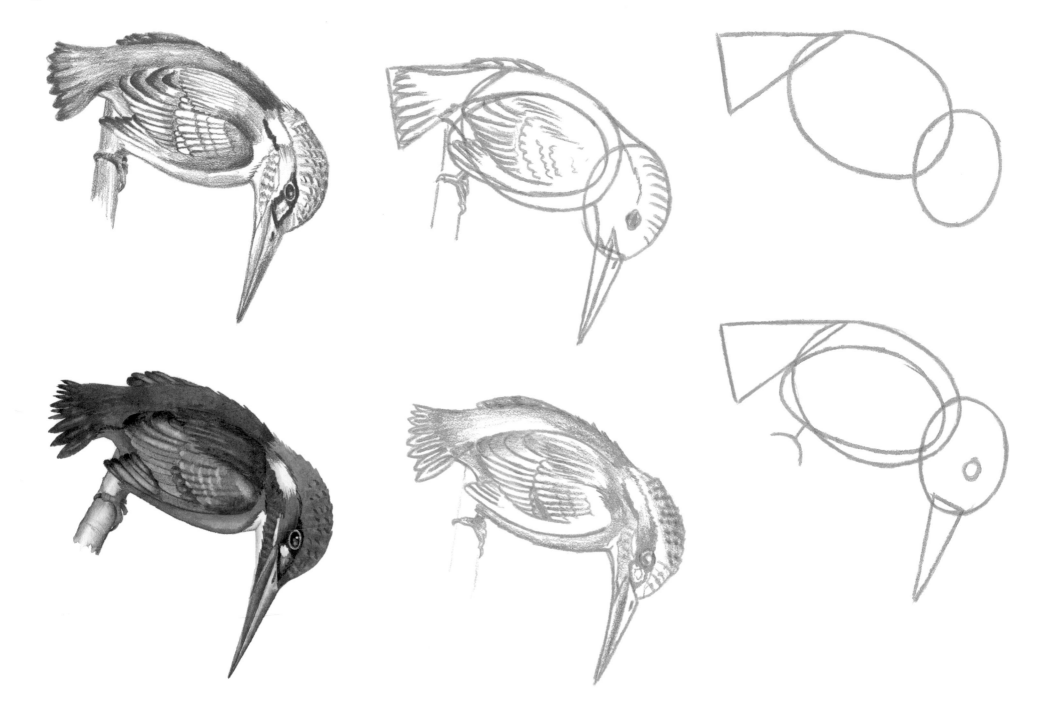

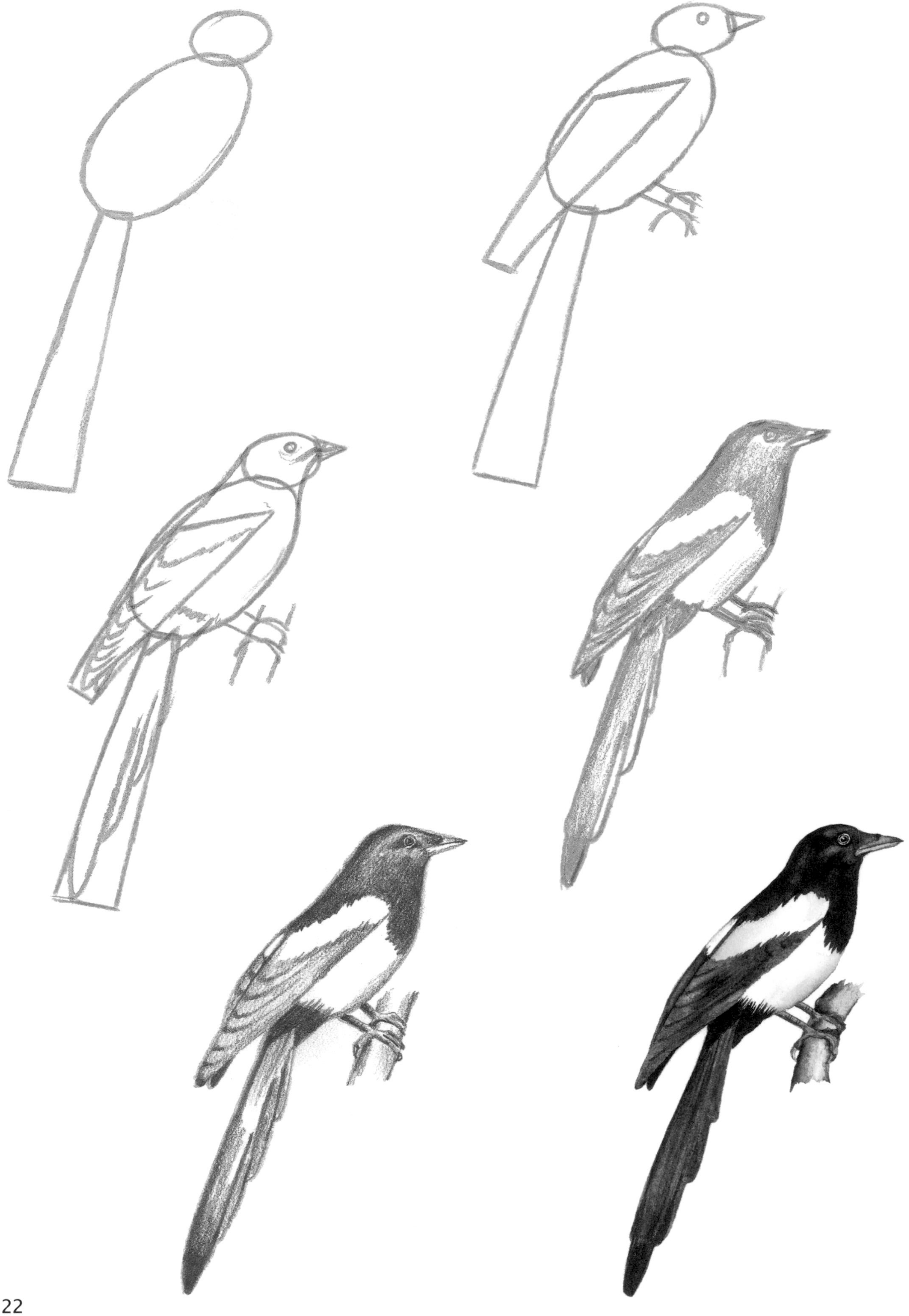

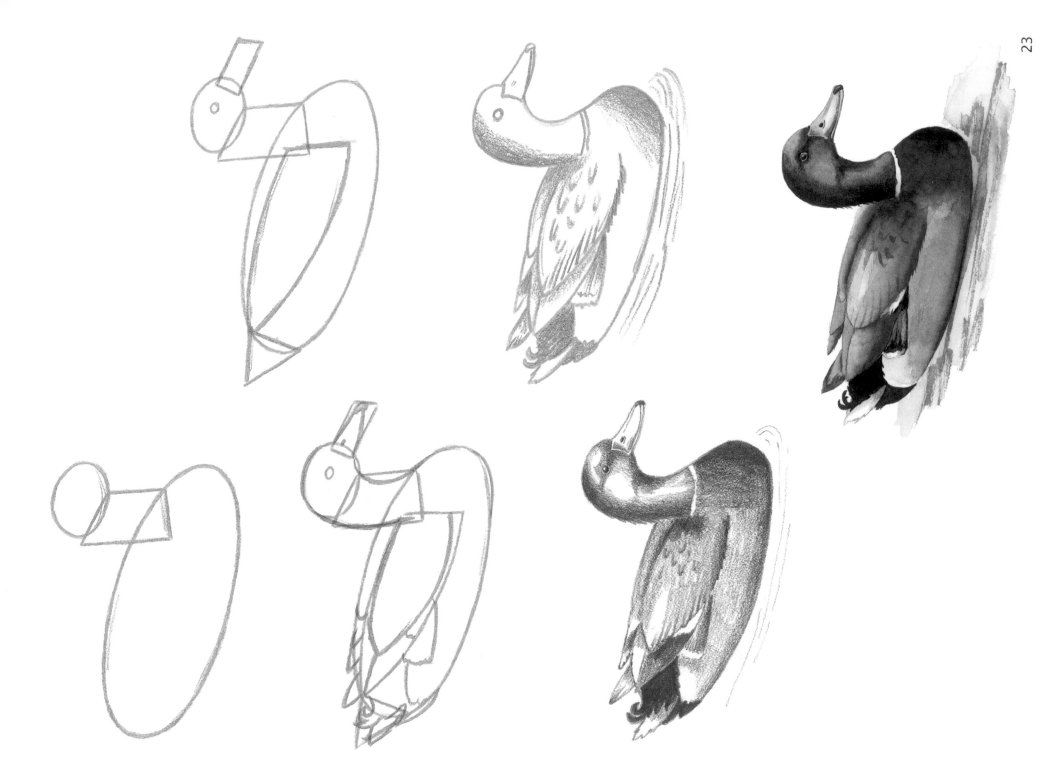

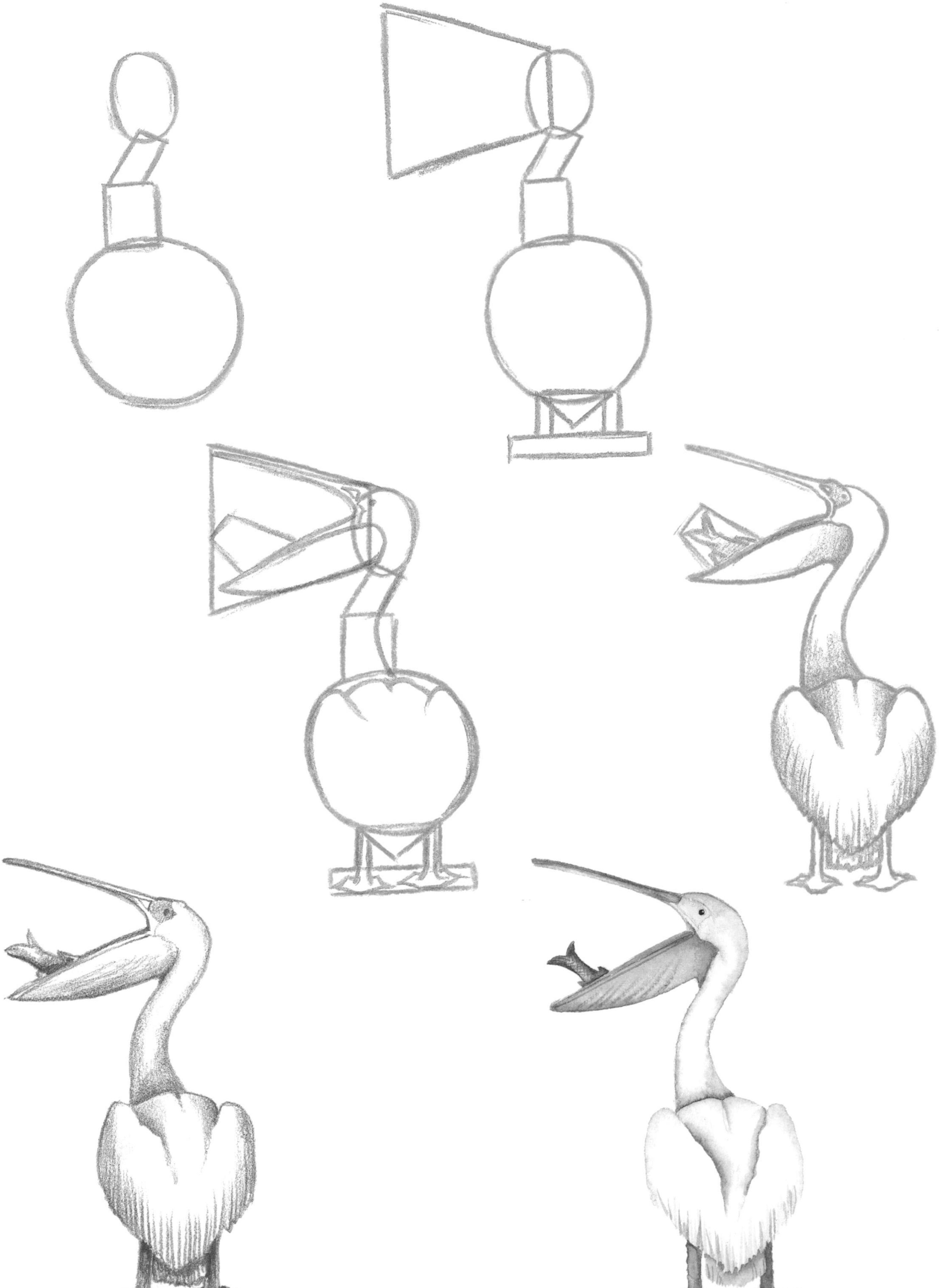

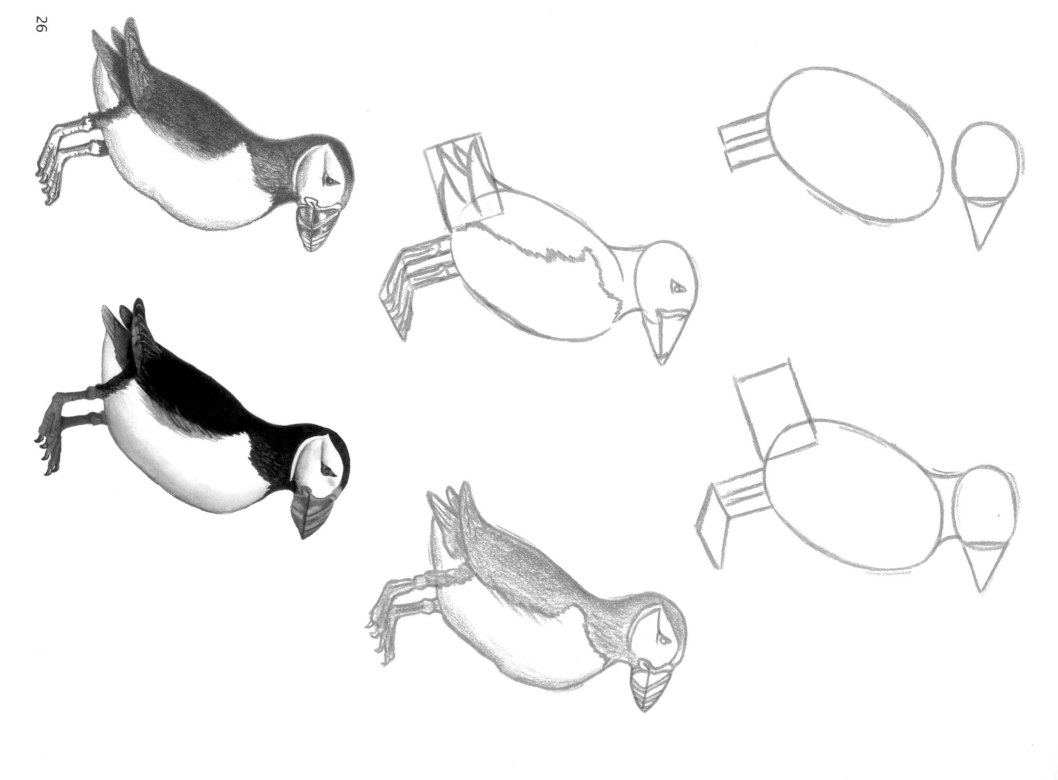

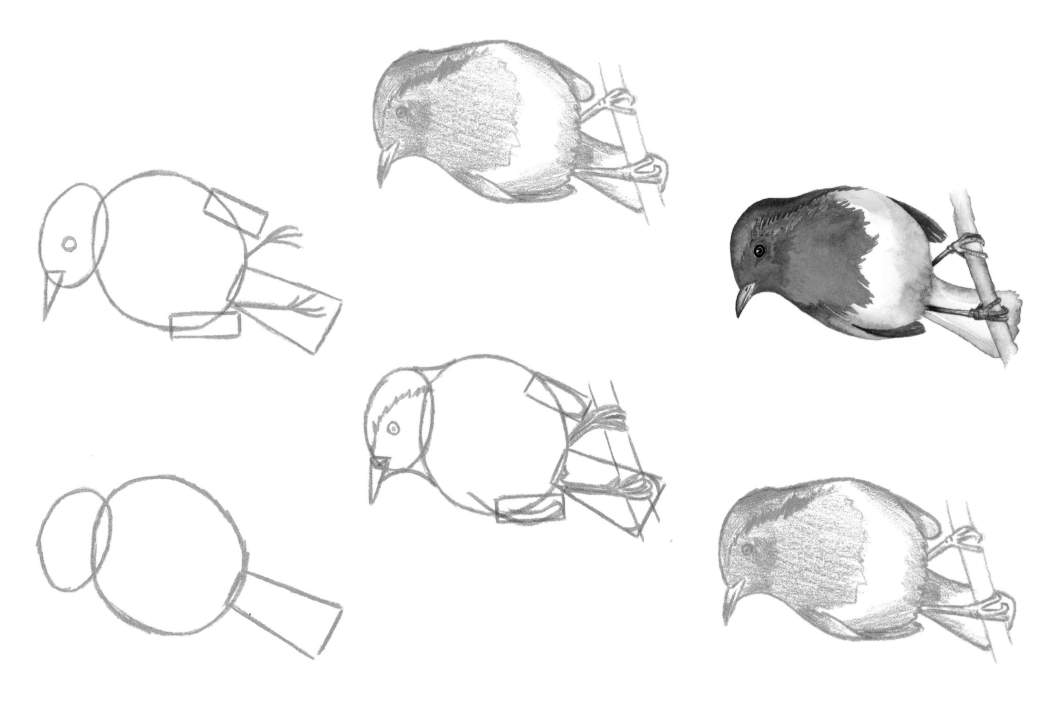

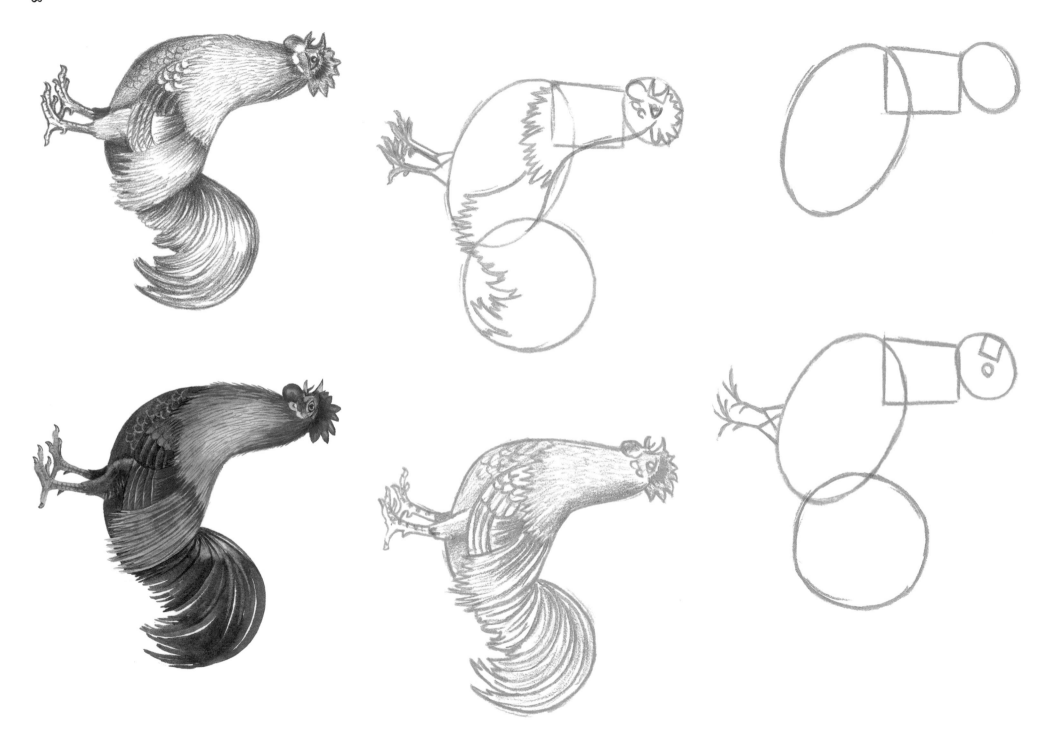

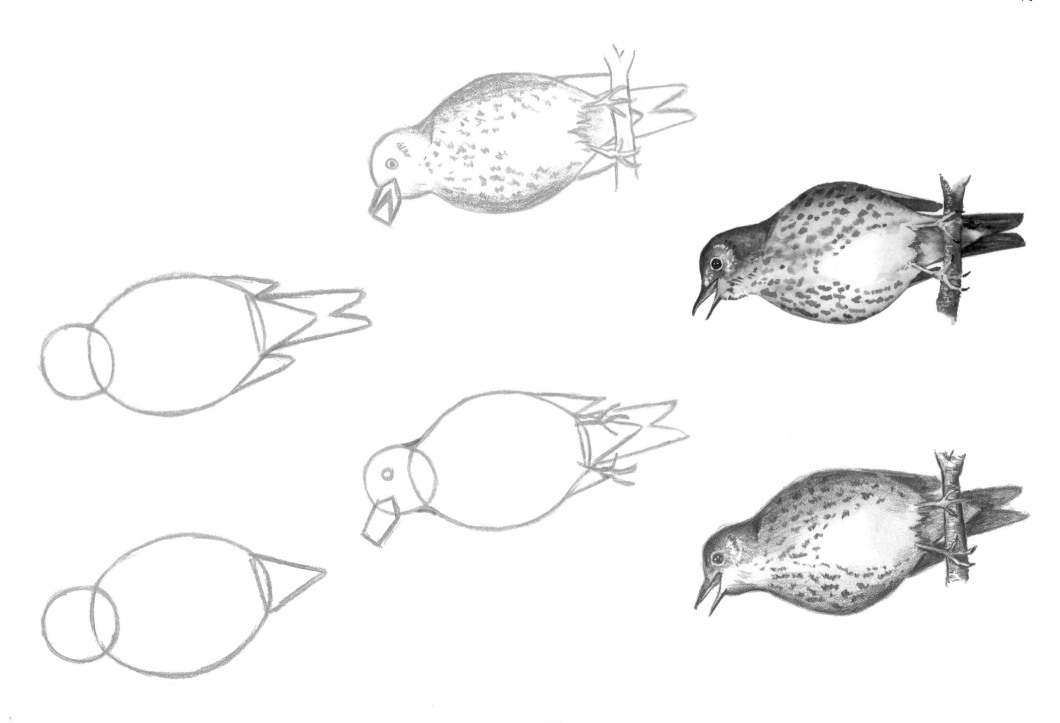

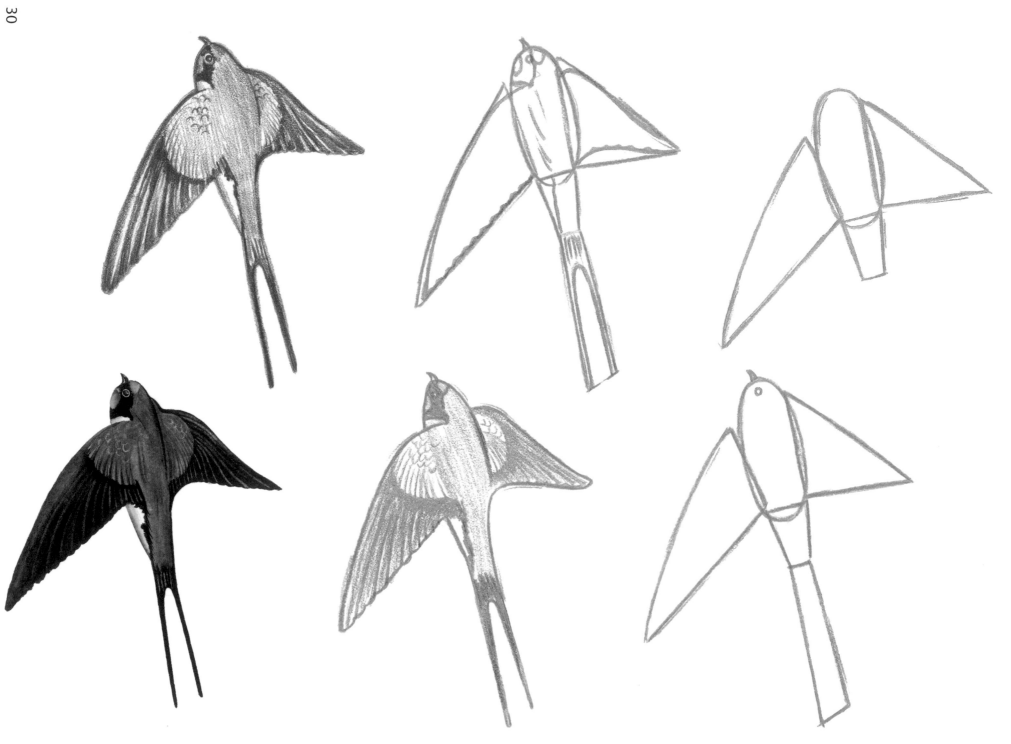

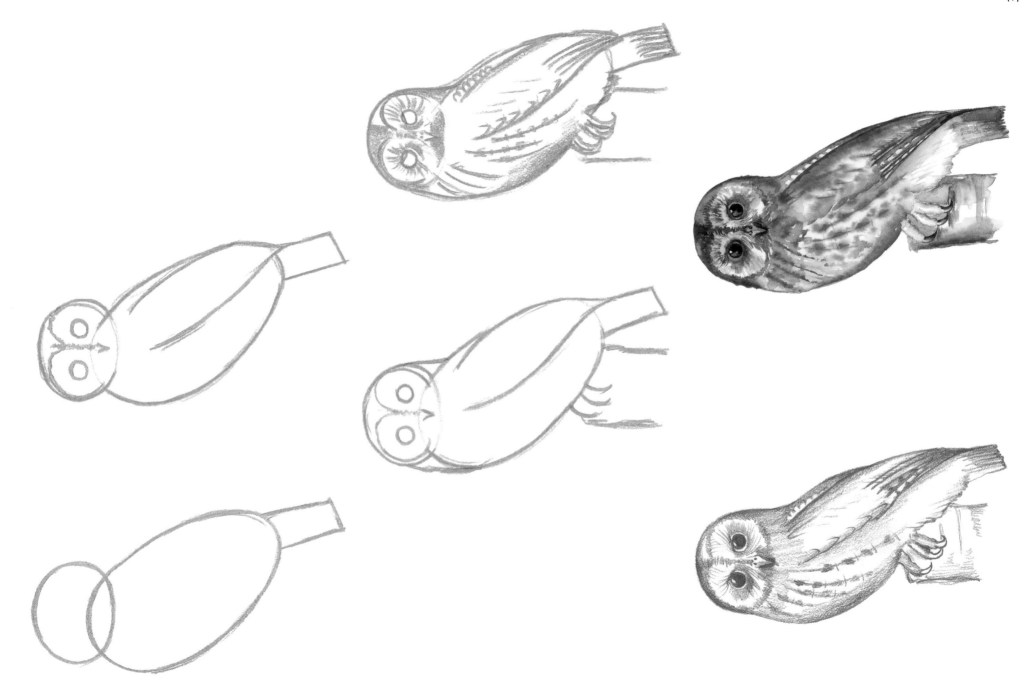

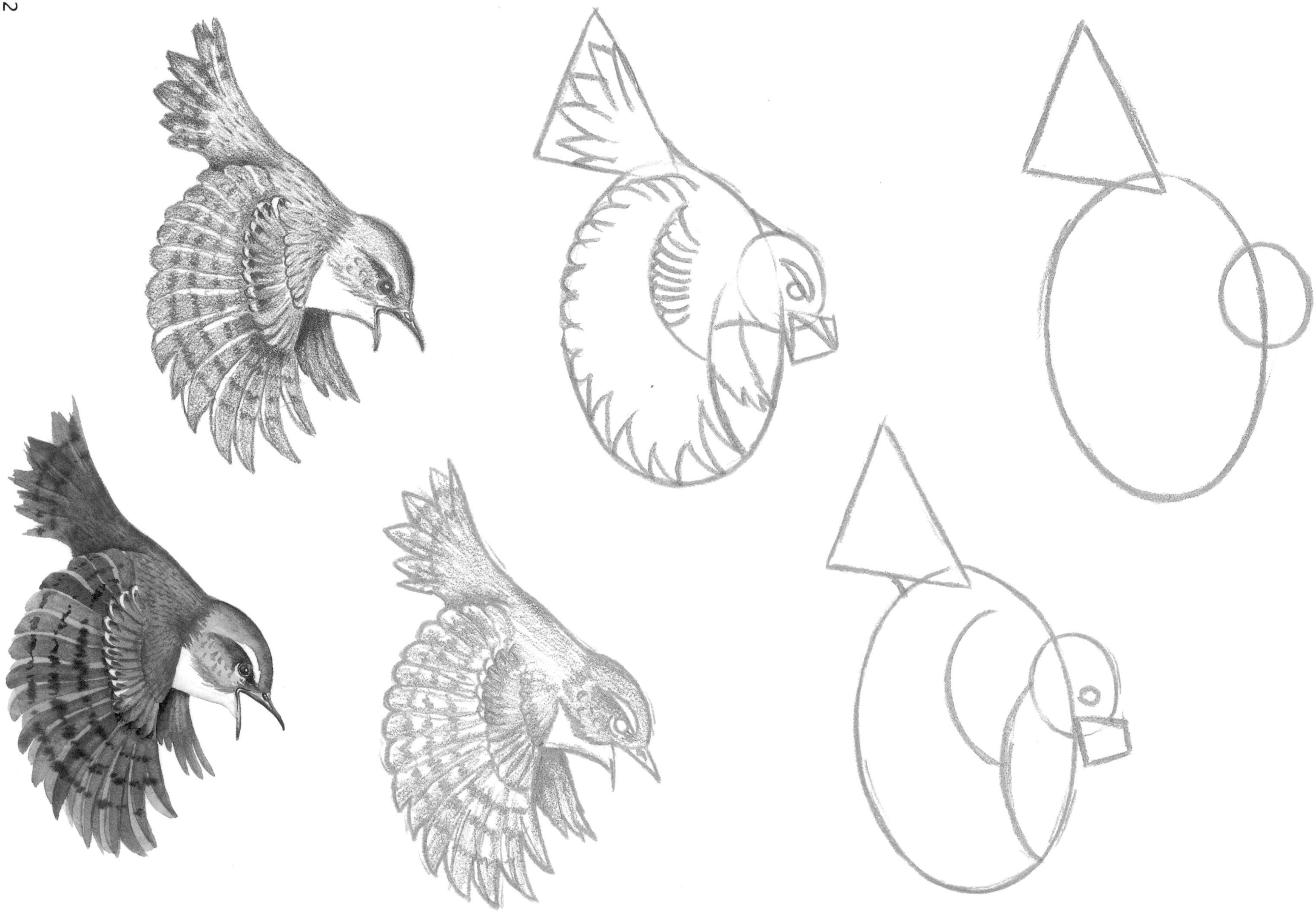